Just Be You, Girl

A Guide to Self-Esteem for All Young Girls Not Living on a Deserted Island

CAROLYN McMAHON

Other than my own, the names and identifying details of all girls quoted in this book have been changed to protect confidentiality.

This book is designed to provide information and motivation. It is sold with the understanding that the author is neither certified nor engaged to render any type of psychological or medical advice. The content of this book is the sole expression and opinion of its author and not intended as a substitute for professional opinion. Please, if you or someone you know needs help, seek the advice of a trusted professional.

Library and Archives Canada Cataloguing in Publication

McMahon, Carolyn, 1964-, author

Just be you, girl : a guide to self-esteem for all young girls not living on a deserted island / Carolyn McMahon.

Includes bibliographical references.
ISBN 978-0-9938856-0-0 (pbk.)

1. Teenage girls — Juvenile literature. 2. Teenage girls — Psychology — Juvenile literature. 3. Teenage girls — Physiology — Juvenile literature. 4. Self-esteem in adolescence — Juvenile literature. I. Title.

HQ798.M35 2014 j305.235'2 C2014-905642-7

Editorial Work:
Catherine Leek of Green Onion Publishing

Cover Art Illustration:
Victoria Yakupova

Interior Design and Formatting:
Kim Monteforte of WeMakeBooks.ca

Cover Design:
Kim Monteforte of WeMakeBooks.ca

Printed in Canada

For Keeley

"Be yourself,
everyone else is taken"
Oscar Wilde

CONTENTS

FRIENDS, FRIENEMIES AND FOES 73

TECHNOLOGY, THE MEDIA & YOU 123

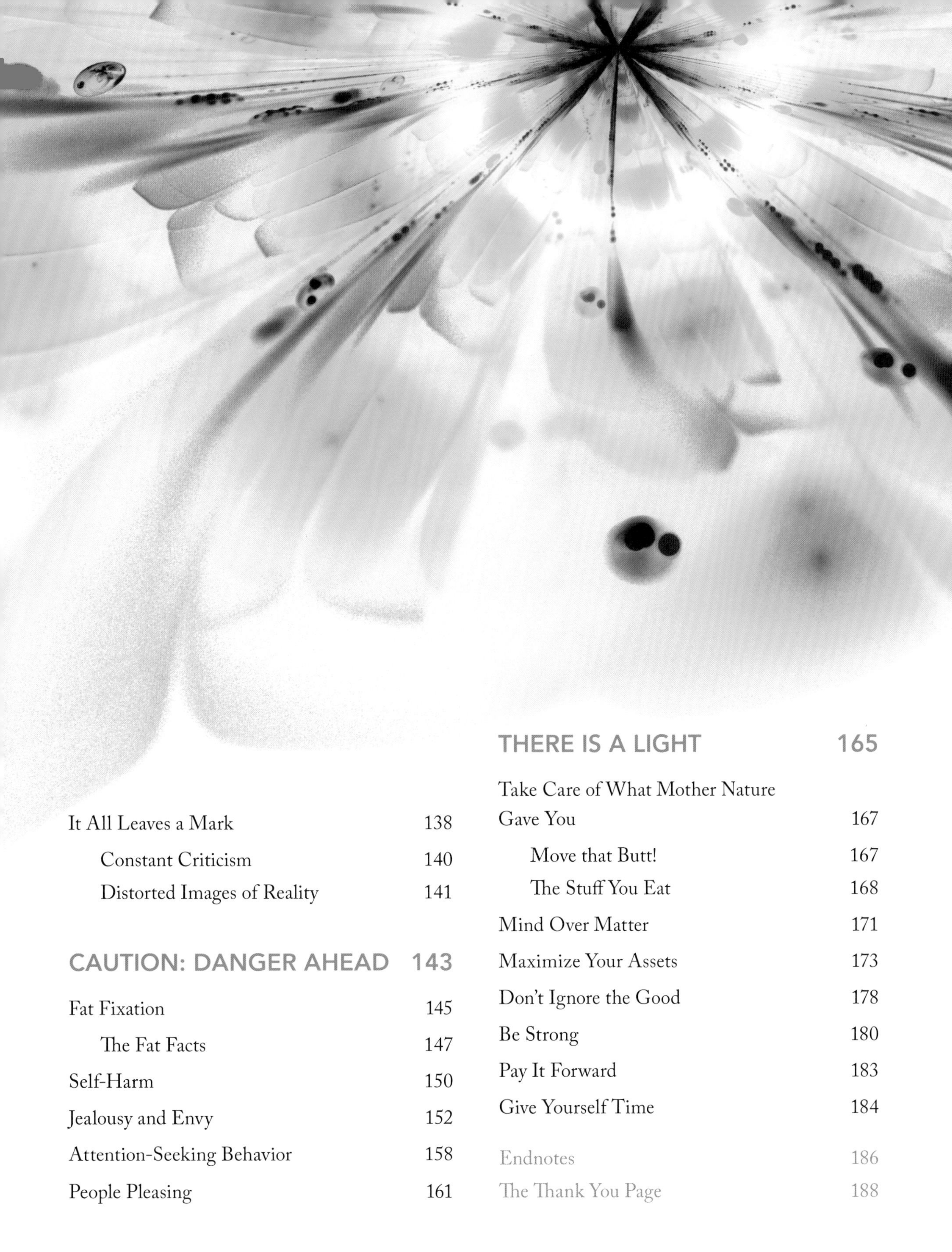

THE GIRL IN THE MIRROR

How do you feel about yourself? What do you think when you look in the mirror? Does it depend on the day?

Seven out of every ten girls believe that they are not good enough or do not measure up in some way.[1] Seven out of ten girls look in the mirror and aren't happy with what they see or with who they are. Are you one of those seven?

Being a girl today can be hard. As a grown up, I can tell you that we have all had to deal with body image issues, jealousies, insecurities and raging hormones. But my generation never had to deal with the constant, over the top, bombardment of media images glamorizing an unattainable perfection. Nor did we have to cope with the 24/7 world of the Internet and cell phones, where everyone is expected to be "on" all the time, and where anyone and everyone feels entitled to judge and report on your every move, which, by the way, is recorded for all time.

You are not only exposed to many more influences, but also at a younger and younger age. Add to this all the classic issues of growing up and you can see how seven in ten girls may believe they are just not good enough.

It can be a tough world to navigate through and many young girls are finding it difficult. Girls just like you. The first thing to know is that, clearly, you are not alone. There is nothing that you have said or thought that other girls are not also saying or thinking.

There is nothing wrong with you; you are not a freak. There is no complaint that you have about your body that thousands of other girls don't have. You are not the only one who thinks she is too fat or too tall or hates the kink in her hair or the freckles on her face or the shade of her skin. You are not the only girl who is being ignored by the boys or, worse, being criticized by them. You are not the only girl who feels isolated, overwhelmed or just plain lost.

When you lay your head on your pillow at night and the tears flow from sadness or anger or confusion, know that there are a lot of other girls with wet pillows as well. This is not meant to say that your problems are not unique or important. They are unique to you and important. Anything that makes you doubt yourself is very important.

It's definitely a tougher world to navigate through, but not impossible. And the truth is, you really have no choice. This is your world. You need to find the strength to not only navigate through, but stand up and be yourself — be the amazing person that you are. No more compromises, no more self-criticism, no more tears. Life is short and you only get one, but luckily you have a lot of power to choose how you want to live yours.

YOUR
POWER

Let's start with a truth.

There is a lot in your life you do not control. You don't get to choose your height. You can't decide your skin color or the size of your feet. You don't pick your family or the circumstances into which you are born. The truth is, some kids get blessed with being born into a safe and loving environment, while others are not so fortunate. It is not a child's choice or fault to be born into a life of violence or poverty. It is not a child's choice or fault to be born ill or alone. There are things in life a person does not get any choice in at all. Some of these things can make life very hard, while some of these things don't need to.

As girls, we tend to add an extra burden to our lives. We tend to hold ourselves up to a notion of perfection that is ever changing and, in reality, doesn't exist at all. We allow the superficial things in our lives, like our height or our weight, to undermine our confidence and prevent us from believing in ourselves and everything that we can be. We allow the world to influence our feelings about ourselves in ways that we don't even recognize. We miss opportunities or fun activities because we are not comfortable with ourselves. We compare ourselves constantly to those around us instead of embracing who we are as individuals. In short, we are often our own worst enemies.

"I feel ugly and stupid because the guy I've had a crush on for two years told me I am ugly and stupid."

Think back to when you were a toddler. You never felt ugly or stupid. You were just happy to be fed and dry, and plopped in front of the TV for a little *Teletubbies*. So what's going on now? How did it all change?

You might think it's obvious where your feelings are coming from. "I feel ugly and stupid because the guy I've had a crush on for two years told me I am ugly and stupid." Okay, fair enough, that's pretty obvious.

But how come you don't just tell that guy to take a flying leap? Why do you assume that what he says is correct? And more to the point, why do you even care?

No one likes to be put down. No matter how confident you are, it's still a jolt. But if you automatically accept that guy's opinion instead of just thinking that he is a creep for saying it, then something else is going on. He has the *power* because he is playing on the insecurities and the poor self-image that you already have about yourself. It's time to take some of that power back.

You may not have a choice over everything in your life, but you do have the choice over how you see yourself. It is time to realize that you are not defined by how you look or an embarrassing moment in your life. You are not defined by whether you are popular with the boys at school, or invited to a particular party. You are defined by you. You are defined by the messages you tell yourself. You may not have the power over all that life hands you, but you have this power. Use it.

Sometimes, no matter how strong you try to be, the external pressures of life are too much. We can't always make changes on our own. If you are in a bad situation where you are being hurt or thinking of hurting yourself, you need to reach out. Tell a trusted adult, tell a teacher, tell a good friend. Shout it from the rooftops if you need someone to hear you because you deserve to be heard. And don't listen to anyone who tells you that you aren't worth it, even if you are thinking that yourself. Life can be so much more than you are experiencing right now and you deserve a great one!

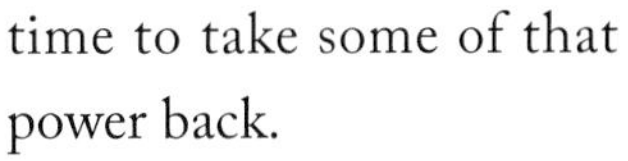

WHAT NO BOOK CAN DO

To be fair, I want to say right up front what this book is not. This book is not a set of easy-to-follow rules on how you should do things in order to be happy and confident. It was not written to tell you how to dress, how to do your hair, what makeup you can wear or what kind of friends you should have. In fact, this book tries very hard not to make any decisions for you.

First of all, you probably have enough rules in your life as it is. You don't need any book giving you more rules. Besides, how could one book tell you what to do in every situation? Do you realize how many decisions you make in a day? Probably not; who keeps track of those things? But let me tell you, it is a lot. What to eat, what to wear, who to sit next to in the lunch room, what activities to get involved in, what to buy your friend for her birthday, what to watch on TV, which music to listen to, … phew! The list of decisions on any one day is exhausting; over a whole lifetime it would be beyond enormous. Besides, every girl is different. That is what makes us all so awesome. The decisions one girl may face will be different than those faced by another girl. And the answer that makes sense for one girl might not work for another. It's your life, so it has to be your choice.

The purpose of this book is simply to get you to open your eyes to the world around you, to understand how your world can affect the feelings you have for yourself, the feelings you have for others and the decisions you make.

Right now, you have tons of influences pressuring and shaping your every decision and every thought. Some of these you might not recognize, many more you might not understand and most you can't control. But you can control the way you react to them. Just as you can choose to make yourself feel bad by always concentrating on negative things, you can choose to make yourself feel better about yourself by learning how to focus on the positive things.

Think about it. If you told a girl every day of her life that she was not good enough or pretty enough, or thin enough, then soon she would start to believe it. You would never do that to someone else, because you are not mean. Yet, many girls will do that to themselves — always telling themselves that they fall short in some way, actually choosing to make themselves feel bad.

Think about it. If you told a girl every day of her life that she was not good enough or pretty enough, or thin enough, then soon she would start to believe it. You would never do that to someone else, because you are not mean. Yet, many girls will do that to themselves — always telling themselves that they fall short in some way, actually choosing to make themselves feel bad.

Why do we do this to ourselves? There are lots of reasons, and hopefully you will find some help in these pages to understand some of them, to help you discover why you think and say things to yourself that make you feel as though you are not as good as everyone else. And maybe you will begin to understand how you hold the power to change those negative feelings so that you see yourself as the truly amazing girl that you are.

If you say the choice is mine, why do you give so much advice?

Before I printed this book, I showed it to someone who said that it may be too preachy because it gives a lot of advice. The reason I do this is simple — it's because my daughter asked me to.

My daughter, a young girl just like you, is also feeling all of the insecurities, anger, sadness and confusion that may be affecting you. So even though I talk with her a lot, I wanted to write something that she could refer to when she was feeling bad or sad or mad — a thought here or a story there — just something that may help her work through these issues. She is the one who asked, "You are going to give actual advice aren't you? You aren't just going to say that it is normal to feel this way? Girls need some actual suggestions on what to do!"

So that is why there is so much advice in here, compiled from the thoughts and wisdom of many women. The suggestions are ours, but the choice is always yours.

TWO REALLY BAD WORDS

If only my eyes were green, or my hair was blonde. If only I was taller or thinner (or, better yet, both). If only I were prettier. If only, I didn't snort when I laugh or if I hadn't accidently farted during that science class. Then my life would be perfect.

If only — two of life's cruelest words. Don't worry, you are not alone in wishing you could change just that one little thing about yourself. Young and old, women throughout the ages have wasted a lot of precious time and shed more than a few tears because of the dreaded *if onlys.*

The list of *if onlys* can be endless. *If only I didn't wear glasses, if only I didn't have so many pimples, if only I were smarter, if only I were someone else, if only, if only, if only ... then everything would be great forever.*

There are two problems with thinking this way.

The first is that not everything about you can be changed, no matter how much you wish it. Some things just have to be accepted. The longer you spend thinking about the *if onlys,* the longer it will be before you can begin accepting yourself for who you actually are.

The second problem is that there is no end to the *if onlys*. Once you slay one, another pops up like the snakes on Medusa's head. As soon as one thing works out just the way you want it, it is not long before you start to focus on a different obstacle, something else that is standing in your way to feeling truly good about yourself.

Answer this question. When was the last time you felt truly amazing and confident about yourself with no *if onlys* lurking in the back of your mind? You are probably thinking about things you want to change about yourself right now while reading this — right at this very second? Seriously, stop it!

Every moment of time you spend dumping on yourself is a moment that you have chosen to make yourself feel bad. Think about it. You have chosen to put your thoughts and energy into making yourself feel bad. Doesn't that sound like an incredible waste of time?

I don't know what is wrong this year. I am jealous or angry or sad most of the time. My friends are changing, the boys in my school are changing, everything is changing.

I have always hated my looks. I have always been taller and bigger than all of the other girls. I always thought that if I wasn't so tall then everything would be good. Now most of the girls in my class are almost as tall as me, but I still hate my looks. The other girls are all so thin and pretty, and I will never be that thin.

My mom says that I am just not built that way and that I am beautiful in my own right, but she doesn't understand. It can be really embarrassing to be different. Especially when the other girls swap clothes and stuff and I can't because their clothes won't fit me. I would give anything if I could just look exactly like them.

And there is other stuff this year too. I've always had lots of friends and been popular. But even that is changing this year. My best friend doesn't even seem to notice if I am around anymore. I don't know why things have changed so much between us. We always used to have a lot of fun, but now she "forgets" to invite me to things and it makes me feel worthless.

I'm just tired of feeling sad all of the time. I can't wait for this year to be done.

— L

HOW MEAN ARE YOU?

In order to think more positively about yourself, you have to begin by being honest about the negative messages you tell yourself. In other words, how mean are you — to yourself? That's right — your messages. Not what anyone else says about you — only what you tell yourself. What someone else may say about you loses power if you don't believe it yourself. Whether someone says something good or bad about you, it's what you believe and say to yourself that affects how you feel about you.

For example, if someone tells you that "you are the stupidest girl in the world" then you might choose to believe that you are stupid. You might even think you have proof that you are stupid because you don't get "A"s on math tests like all your friends. So it is easy to believe what others say — to let them define you and tell you how you should feel about yourself. That's a lot of power you have just given away.

You can keep that power for yourself. You don't have to believe the negatives, the stereotypes or the media messages that tell you how you should be. You can believe the best about yourself.

Let's face it. None of us is perfect, but none of us is simple either. We can't be defined by just one aspect of ourselves. You may not get "A"s in math, but you are sure to have knowledge in many other areas if you just open your eyes to yourself. And if you allow yourself to see the value in all these other things that you are, then the power that others have to define you will diminish.

Everyone has doubts about themselves. Everyone has insecurities. Whether it's the shape of your eyes, the shade of your skin, the type of house you live in or one of a million other things, the problem comes when you allow someone, or something, to use those insecurities to make you feel bad about yourself. "You are going to fail in life because you are stupid."

If you allow yourself to believe these negatives, you will actually repeat them to yourself. "You're right. I am stupid." At this point, you are actually the one saying those mean things to yourself. Take a moment and think about it. You control what you think about yourself.

Okay, okay. I know what you are saying right now. "Nice thought, but it is not that easy to control how I feel about myself. I just feel the way I feel!" You're right, it is not that easy. Lots of things influence how we feel about ourselves, and it's not easy to always ignore them or rise above them. Don't worry about that right now. For now, just concentrate on how you actually feel about yourself. How hard are you on yourself?

WHAT'S YOUR SELF-TALK SOUND LIKE?

A good exercise is to keep track over the course of one day, how many time you say/think something negative to yourself. It might be an "if only" or it might be worded differently, but the result is the same. It is a message that makes you feel not particularly good about yourself.

For example:

If only I was like her.

I am fat.

If only I was allowed to wear what the other girls wear.

I hate my hair. I wish it flowed long and straight.

Be honest. This exercise is for no one but you. No one else will know what you are thinking. If you want, write down your messages as you go through the day. Once you see your list in writing you might be amazed at how many negative messages you allow yourself during a day.

Why is this important?

The actual specifics of the list are not important. That is, what you are actually upset about on any given day is not the thing. Today you may be upset because you think you are too fat. Tomorrow you might feel like a loser because you don't have that new phone that all the kids have. The point is, when you allow yourself to view your life in negatives instead of positives there is no end to the negatives that you will see.

You may be shocked at how unfair you are to yourself. I bet you will discover that you say things to yourself that you would never say or even think about someone else. Yet you have no problem being that hard on yourself.

The important thing is to see for yourself exactly how many times you dump on yourself in one day. If you are honest with yourself, you will be surprised by the amount of time you spend each day making yourself feel bad; the amount of time you spend thinking about the *if onlys.*

And consider this idea. There is only so much time in each day. You can only process so many thoughts and do so many things in any given time period. The more time you waste on negative energy, the less time you have for positive energy to flow through your day. This means you have less time to try new things, engage new people or just have fun. You are robbing yourself of positive time and experiences.

Desiring change is not a bad thing. Wanting to achieve more is not a bad thing. Wanting to take better care of yourself, look nicer or get better grades are all great goals to have.

It is how you frame your thoughts that's important. Positive change comes from positive messages. Negative messages undermine your self-esteem and rarely result in positive long-term changes.

Giving Up the Power

One in every five girls will avoid giving her opinion when she feels bad about the way she looks.[1]

I was in about grade four the first time I really became self-conscious about my body. A friend and I were having a sleepover at another friend's house. So there were three of us. The mom at the friend's house where we were sleeping had bought us all matching PJs. It was a nice thought, but she bought the PJs at a kid's store and they only went up to a certain size. I was already tall by then and already filling out a bit. It hadn't really bothered me before. I never even really thought about it. But when she gave us our PJs, mine didn't fit. I mean, not even passable. So there were my two friends with their new pink PJs and me wearing a pair borrowed from my friend's mom. I felt like such a loser.

— M

WHAT THE *BLEEP* HAPPENED?

Remember when you were younger — not baby young (it's hard to remember those times) — but little girl young. Remember when you would go to school in your PJs, or wear your most favorite princess dress to the park. Remember when you just did and wore what made you feel good. You didn't care if anyone else wanted to wear one purple sock with one orange sock over green striped tights; you just went for it, because you liked it. You made your choices based on what made you feel good, not by comparing yourself to others. You had no idea what being *popular* meant. You didn't see yourself as too short or too fat. You just hopped right into the sandbox, princess dress and all, and started laughing with everyone else. Those were pretty good times. Don't you miss those times a little?

But then something changed. What was it?

Well you got older. You started noticing the things around you. Suddenly, you began to notice the differences between you and your friends. At about the same time, your body started changing — a lot. Small differences between you and your friends were becoming bigger differences. On top of all that, your world started to expand. All of a sudden there were a lot more people in your life — teachers, coaches, classmates, all of whom began to influence the way you thought of yourself. And as if that was not enough, *Dora the Explorer* was replaced with reality television, music videos, YouTube, teen movies, fashion magazines and a ton of other captivating images, all inviting you to a grow up and join in a brand new world.

So here you are. You're growing, your body is changing and you find yourself surrounded by an exciting, yet at times scary, new world. It's a lot to take in — a fantastically huge amount of stuff to take in — all in a very short period of time. This may likely be one of the hardest periods of your life to steer through. So take a breath, and give yourself a break. It is going to be overwhelming at times. You are going to get confused at times. But understand this, you are not alone. Millions of young girls are going through the same thing you are at this very moment.

But why have you all of a sudden become so much more self-conscious about yourself? Why are

This is the day when I stopped feeling pretty. I am Japanese and my eyes are sort of almond shaped. When I was young, I was always told what a pretty little girl I was, so I always felt very pretty and never gave any special thought to my eyes. But one day when I was a bit older, maybe grade five, I was at my friend's house and we were playing around with some makeup and she said something like, "You can't wear eye shadow as good because your eyes are too small." That was all it took.

— M

you all of a sudden so unsure about what to wear and how to do your hair? Why do you just not feel as comfortable in your own skin anymore? Is it the changes your body is going through? Partly.

There is a lot going on with your body right now, and not all of it is happily anticipated. But puberty can often end up taking the blame for every thought or emotion a girl has at this age. And girls are often told not to worry about things at this stage of their life. Maybe you have heard that *you will outgrow it*, it is *just your hormones*, these feelings you are having *won't last* or, worse yet, that they're *not real*. While it is true that puberty can affect many of your feelings and that your body does experience significant change right through to young adulthood, it is more than just this. Many girls continue to be uncomfortable with themselves well beyond puberty, right through adulthood. If it were just puberty affecting a young woman's self-confidence, then the cosmetic, diet and plastic surgery industries wouldn't be billion dollar businesses (and growing every year)!

Having said that, however, the physical and hormonal changes you are going through at this stage in your life are major and shouldn't be underestimated by anyone, including yourself. It is very important for you that you understand all of these changes. Nothing is scarier than when you don't understand what is happening to your body, especially if it is not happening to all of your friends at the same time.

This book is not a book about puberty. However, there are lots of great books out there that can prepare you or answer your questions. Just be careful about where you get your information. I know the

Internet is quicker, easier and cheaper than going to a bookstore, but there are a lot of jokesters and less than intelligent strangers out there who may not be the best ones to turn to when needing to understand the finer points on menstruation. Plus, who knows what will come back when you input questions like, "How big will my breasts get?" or "How much hair growth is normal?" So, not to knock the Internet, but if you want to use it, make very sure the site you are referencing is credible or ask a trusted adult to help you find the information you need.

So, is puberty important? Yup. But there are also a lot of other factors influencing you right now and they are just as important. And just as you would take the time to learn about what's going on with puberty, you need to learn, or at least really pay attention to, all of these other things in your life that can affect how you feel about yourself and the world around you.

Consider this thought. If you lived alone on a deserted island your whole life (right from birth, before you could be influenced by any outside factors), how concerned would you be with the shape of your legs? Probably not very much. You would just be happy that you had two healthy legs that got you around the island. You wouldn't think their shape should be any different than they were.

Now consider this. What if you moved alone to the deserted island later in life, after being exposed to boys' opinions, magazine covers and MTV videos? How concerned would you be with the shape of your legs then? I am guessing again, probably not very much. Because, alone on the island, you don't have to compare yourself to anyone else. What you will be most grateful for is that you have two healthy legs to get you around and up the coconut trees.

If it were just puberty affecting a young woman's self-confidence, then the cosmetic, diet and plastic surgery industries wouldn't be billion dollar businesses (and growing every year)!

When I was in grade six, the girl that stood out most in the class was Jessica. To me, she was the "perfect girl." She always seemed so happy and everyone liked her. Life just looked easy for her. I guess I was a little jealous of that. So I got it in my head that I wanted to be more like her or, better yet, exactly like her. I just assumed back then that to be like someone, you just had to look like them.

So when school got out that year, I vowed to spend my whole summer getting to be as much like Jessica as possible. She had long curly dark hair and was small, like china-doll small. So I started to grow my hair as long as possible and I spent forever every morning curling it so it would look like hers. And then once I had spent forever curling it, I didn't want to go into our pool because it would ruin all my hard work. I didn't want to do anything that would ruin it. I basically just sat around a lot that summer. I also refused to eat anything more than necessary, trying to shrink my body to the smallest size possible. This was really hard since my parents allowed way more treats in the summer than during the normal year (I really missed my s'mores).

Anyway, finally the first day of grade seven arrived and I couldn't wait for everyone to see the brand new me! I took extra-long that morning, making sure that I looked "just right." I'm not exactly sure what I expected to happen, but I didn't expect what happened next. I will never forget coming around the side of the school and running right into a group of my friends all hugging in that "so great to be back together" way. And there in the middle was Jessica. I couldn't believe my eyes. China-doll Jessica had grown four inches, filled out and had cut her long hair into a short pixie with an added pink streak running through it. I didn't look at all like Jessica anymore.

And on top of it all, my new looks didn't instantly give me Jessica's life, like I had hoped. I still had my same life and Jessica was still Jessica — still always pretty happy. It took me a long time to figure out that was just Jessica. It was just the person she was. I wish I had figured that out before I wasted a whole hot summer without swimming or s'mores!

— T

But you don't live on a deserted island. You live in the real world, surrounded by lots and lots of people with lots and lots of opinions. Opinions about everything from what music is best, to who is the greatest dancer, to what shape a girl's legs should be. This makes life interesting. There are so many different images and ideas to explore. This can be a great thing. But it can also be a dangerous thing.

29% of girls won't go to the beach, pool or sauna because they feel badly about the way they look.[2]

You see, everything and everyone you come in contact with influences you in some way. Sometimes you don't even realize it is happening. It is so subtle that you don't realize that over time your thoughts about yourself or others have changed because of what you have been exposed to.

Some of these influences can be very positive — the coach who encourages you to try out for the volleyball team, the teacher who opens your eyes to art, the new friend who shares your love of running.

But some of these influences can make you feel bad about yourself, lose your confidence and become angry. Although you might not do it on purpose, as your world expands, you start to measure yourself against all the other people you see, all the images that bombard you daily, all of the opinions you come in contact with. And it can seem impossible to measure up and exhausting just trying to keep on top of it all. Somewhere along the line, little by little, you might start to become sad and angry at yourself. You may try to *fix* all the things you think are wrong with you. But you can't because there are always more things depending on what the latest opinion is. And you get angry at the things you can't fix and you blame your God or Mother Nature or your parents or someone, anyone, for all those things that are wrong with you. Pretty soon (and you may not even be aware of this), you spend more of your time telling yourself what is wrong with you then what is right with you. And that is not the way it should be.

Once you start living your life to someone else's ideal, then you are lost. You will forever be focusing on the negative. Do not let the world around you control you. Understand how your world influences you so that you can choose to embrace the positive, reject the preposterous and focus on what you are. You are a truly remarkable girl!

MEASURING UP

What makes you unhappy?

I'm fat.

I'm ugly.

My breasts are too big.

My breasts are too small.

I'm too tall.

I'm too short.

My hair is thin.

My arms are hairy.

My nose is too big.

I don't look like the other girls in my class.

My thighs are too fat.

I hate my pimples.

The hair on my legs is dark and thick.

My feet are big.

My sister is prettier than me.

I'm not allowed to wear what all my friends wear.

This is just a random sampling of the answers I received when I asked girls what makes them unhappy. This is not a scientific survey. Although each and every girl was beautiful (as defined by me) and healthy, nearly all the girls I asked tended to focus on external traits of beauty as defining their happiness/unhappiness.

Now to be fair, the girls I spoke with were mostly from comfortable, middle-class backgrounds. Asking this question to young girls in a war-torn country or to those living in poverty or in abusive situations would surely yield different answers. But the truth is, unless facing extreme hardship, many girls (and women) tend to list their looks as one of their top preoccupations.

In extreme cases, a person's unhappiness with their physical appearance can be due to a mental illness known as Body Dysmorphic Disorder (BDD).

Although BDD is extreme, the struggle many young girls have with their looks can lead to low self-esteem. *Self-esteem* reflects a person's overall self-appraisal of their worth. It is defined as confidence and satisfaction in oneself.[4]

Nearly 1 in 3 girls, grades 6-8, often wish they were someone else.[3]

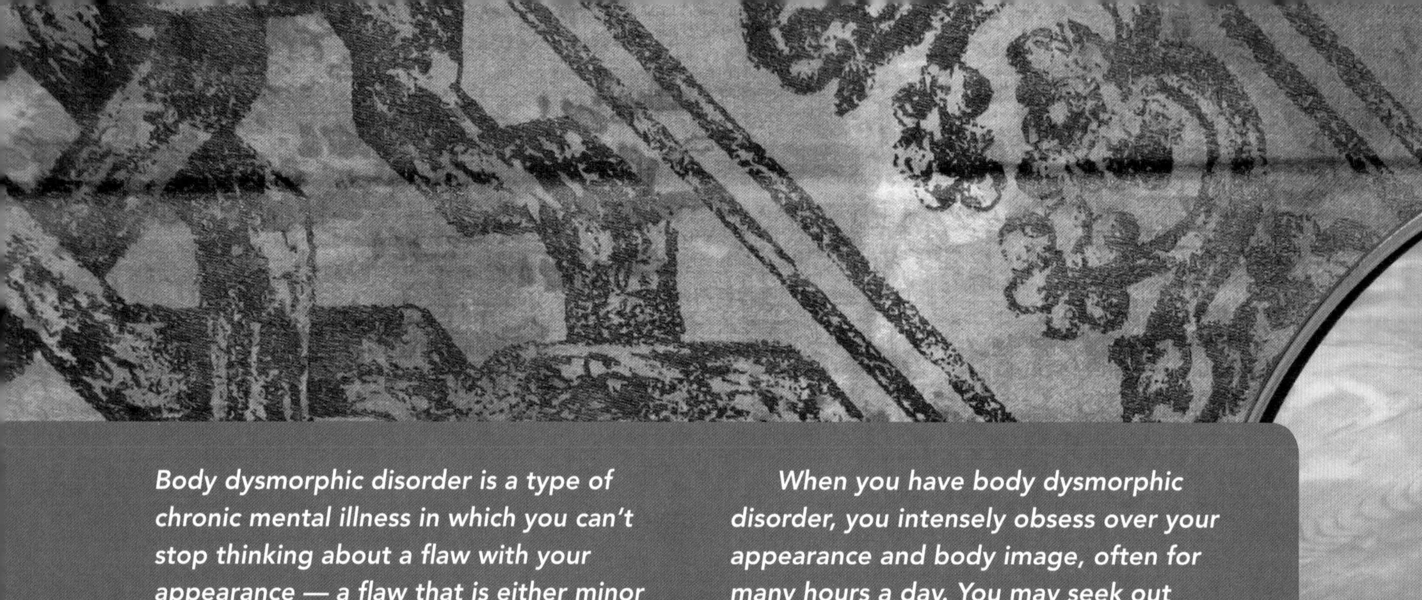

Body dysmorphic disorder is a type of chronic mental illness in which you can't stop thinking about a flaw with your appearance — a flaw that is either minor or imagined. But to you, your appearance seems so shameful that you don't want to be seen by anyone. Body dysmorphic disorder has sometimes been called "imagined ugliness."

When you have body dysmorphic disorder, you intensely obsess over your appearance and body image, often for many hours a day. You may seek out numerous cosmetic procedures to try to "fix" your perceived flaws, but never will be satisfied. Body dysmorphic disorder is also known as dysmorphophobia, the fear of having a deformity.[5]

When you feel good about yourself and your accomplishments, you have good self-esteem. When your self-esteem is healthy, you have a stronger respect for yourself and are more confident and happier with life — all good things! The opposite is true as your self-esteem decreases.

Self-esteem is tied to what's important to you. For example, if the most important thing to you is to become a doctor, then your self-esteem will rise as you do well in school and get accepted into medical school and eventually graduate. You have worked hard and achieved your goal and you feel proud of it. Way to go!

On the other hand, you don't have to achieve a concrete goal to build a strong self-esteem. Sometimes a person is proud of the fact that they will take risks and try new things. Some of the things they try work out and some don't. The satisfaction and self-respect comes from the *trying*.

People don't often feel good about themselves all the time and that's okay. We all go through some hard times where we may lose confidence in ourselves, but an overall positive self-image and self-respect is necessary to a strong, positive and happy life.

Self-Esteem Matters

75% of girls with low self-esteem reported engaging in harmful activities like disordered eating, cutting, bullying, smoking or drinking when feeling badly about themselves.[6]

Why Are We Talking about All This?

- Because when you ask a young girl what she thinks of herself, you are more likely to get a negative answer about some physical quality she doesn't like than you are to get a positive answer about what she is good at or has accomplished.
- Because we live in a culture obsessed with physical beauty, defined by very narrow criteria.
- Because, through media messages, we lie to our girls constantly, telling them they can and should physically improve themselves instead of focusing on all the great things that they are right now.
- Because young girls are set up to fail, trying to obtain a perfection of beauty that doesn't exist.
- Because young girls all over the world are struggling with poor self-esteem and poor body-image issues.

But when you don't respect yourself and all that you have to offer, it can make life very difficult and you can suffer both mentally and physically. You may become depressed, angry, anxious, withdrawn. You may have trouble eating, sleeping or making good choices for yourself. So, self-esteem, the respect that you give yourself, has very real consequences for your life.

No one instinctively knows that they are too tall or too short. You didn't know it in the sandbox and you wouldn't know it if you lived alone on a deserted island. You judge yourself through comparison to others, because of the images you see daily and because of what people tell you. A cruel remark by a boy, coupled with supermodel images, and all of a sudden you don't measure up.

I know that feeling good about your appearance at this age is important. It is important to most females no matter what their age. We all want to feel good about the way we look. No one is suggesting that you should not care about your appearance. It is all in how you balance it with your acceptance of yourself. You want to concentrate on feeling good about *your* look, not obsessing about copying someone else's or, worse yet, trying to measure up to some fantasy of perfection.

If you are always looking to others to approve of you based on how you look, then you will always fall short. If your self-esteem and self-worth are tied to nothing but your appearance, then you are setting yourself up for a very difficult life. It is because there is no perfect look. There is no one right way to look. Beauty is in the eye of the beholder, which means that different people are attracted to different things. So if you are trying to please everyone, it just won't work — you can't be all things to all people. There will always be someone there to criticize something or point out some perceived shortcoming. Plus, the truth is, you have to work with what Mother Nature gave you. Sometimes you might be able to tweak it a bit, but not always. You might not want to be taller than all the other girls, but it is not likely that you are going to be able to change your height. That is just a fact.

So instead of spending countless hours and tears trying to measure up to someone else's standard, you can choose to concentrate on defining and feeling good about your own look, so it is only your approval that you seek when you look in the mirror.

If your self-esteem and self-worth are tied to nothing but your appearance, then you are setting yourself up for a very difficult life.

In grade four I was singled out by the boys in my class for being "different." For me, being "different" means my skin color was not white. My mom is Guyanese and my dad is French Canadian.

I was asked why I was neither "white" nor "black." I told them I was proud to be French-Canadian/Guyanese, and I was proud of my parents, and it had nothing to do with my skin color.

Not knowing how to accept me, they decided to call me Chihuahua. That name stayed with me until my mom intervened.

— M

BEAUTY — THROUGH TIME AND ACROSS OCEANS

Consider this. When you see a cute boy, what makes him so cute to you? Maybe you like brown hair or blonde hair. Maybe you like tall, skinny guys or maybe you are more into a guy with a shorter, muscular build. Who knows? And maybe what first attracted you to that boy had nothing whatsoever to do with his looks. Maybe it was his athletic ability, the way he could make you laugh or how special he made you feel. There are a thousand ways in which a person can be defined.

No doubt the way we look is one of them. The way we express ourselves through our clothes and general appearance says a lot about who we are. And that's great. It can be a lot of fun to experiment with looks and styles, as long as we don't lose ourselves in all the surface stuff. In other words, all style and no substance makes for a very boring life. But as girls, we definitely don't always remember that who we are is made up of so much more than how we look.

Girls (and women) are brutal on themselves. There is not a single body part that escapes our scrutiny — from the thickness of our ankles to the arch of our eyebrows. We relentlessly pick, pluck and process every square inch of ourselves in the pursuit of ideal beauty. But, and here's the rub, what is "ideal beauty?" If you could be ideally beautiful, what would you look like and why? The answer to this question would most certainly depend on when and where you were born.

When you roll your eyes the next time someone tells you that you're beautiful, don't be too quick to assume they are lying. The saying, "beauty is in the eye of the beholder" is absolutely true. Just as you have preferences in what you like to see in others, so too, do others have different opinions of what is beautiful. I know this might not always seem the case. There does seem to be a certain "type" that makes it to the cover of the fashion magazines and beauty advertisements. But is this "ideal" beauty real? Throughout both time and place, the popular concept of what is considered beautiful changes like the wind. The woman you currently see on the cover of your favorite fashion magazine has not always been considered conventionally beautiful and still might not be in many cultures throughout the world.

THROUGH TIME

The Renaissance refers to the time in Europe from the 14th to the 17th Century. During this period, thin was definitely not in. Women would not be considered beautiful if any of their bones were showing. An ideal woman had plenty of soft flesh and thicker arms and legs were a sign of beauty. You can see this ideal reflected in the famous paintings of the time.

Another trend of the time can be seen in the portraits of Queen Elizabeth of England. Women throughout the land would copy the Queen's style, which came to represent beauty itself. During this period, throughout England and Europe, pale skin was considered a feminine ideal — no tanning salons here — the whiter the better. To achieve this look, women would use a cream called "ceruse." Ceruse was made by mixing vinegar and lead. Although it did the trick as far as lightening the skin, it had some nasty side-affects given that lead is one poisonous substance. Lead poisoning could cause everything from hair loss and muscle paralysis to insanity and death.

Italy — Circa 1515

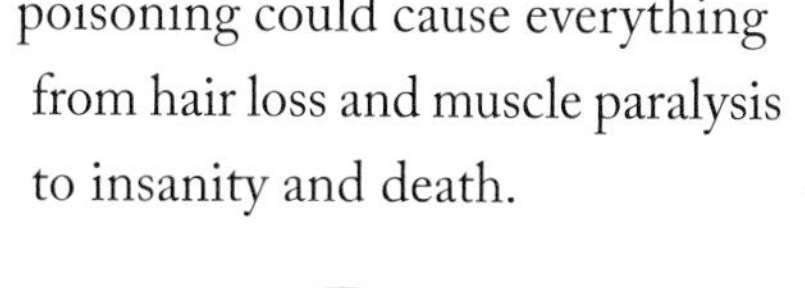

And unlike today, where women would actually be upset to find their hairline receding, women of this period actually plucked their hairline in order to make their forehead seem higher — sort of the reverse of our modern day hair extensions.

It is not until relatively recently that ultra-skinny has become associated with beauty. In paintings, pictures and literature throughout the ages, girls of beauty were often described as plump.

In Louisa May Alcott's *Little Women*, written in 1869, the following passage describes Margaret, the oldest daughter.

> *Margaret, the eldest of the four, was sixteen, and very pretty, being plump and fair, with large eyes, plenty of soft brown hair, a sweet mouth, and white hands, of which she was rather vain.*

As an aside, if you have not yet read this book, you might want to give it a try. Set in the 1800s, it is the story of four sisters and the paths their lives take while each struggles to find her place in the world. I know you might think that this would be a very old and dull book, especially since there is not a vampire anywhere to be seen, but it is really a great story. And although the girls in the story live in another time, faced with a completely different set of rules, they are still just like you — young girls curious about the world around them and all that it has to offer.

Up until about the mid-1900s (which may seem like ancient times to you, but is really not that long ago), women were celebrated for their curves.

In the 1950s, Marilyn Monroe was considered one of the most beautiful women in North America. At about five-foot-five, Marilyn had a beautiful curvaceous body. The common term back then was to refer to a woman with curves like Marilyn's as having an "hour glass" figure.

MEN WOULDN'T LOOK AT ME WHEN I WAS SKINNY

Skinny GIRLS ARE NOT GLAMOUR GIRLS

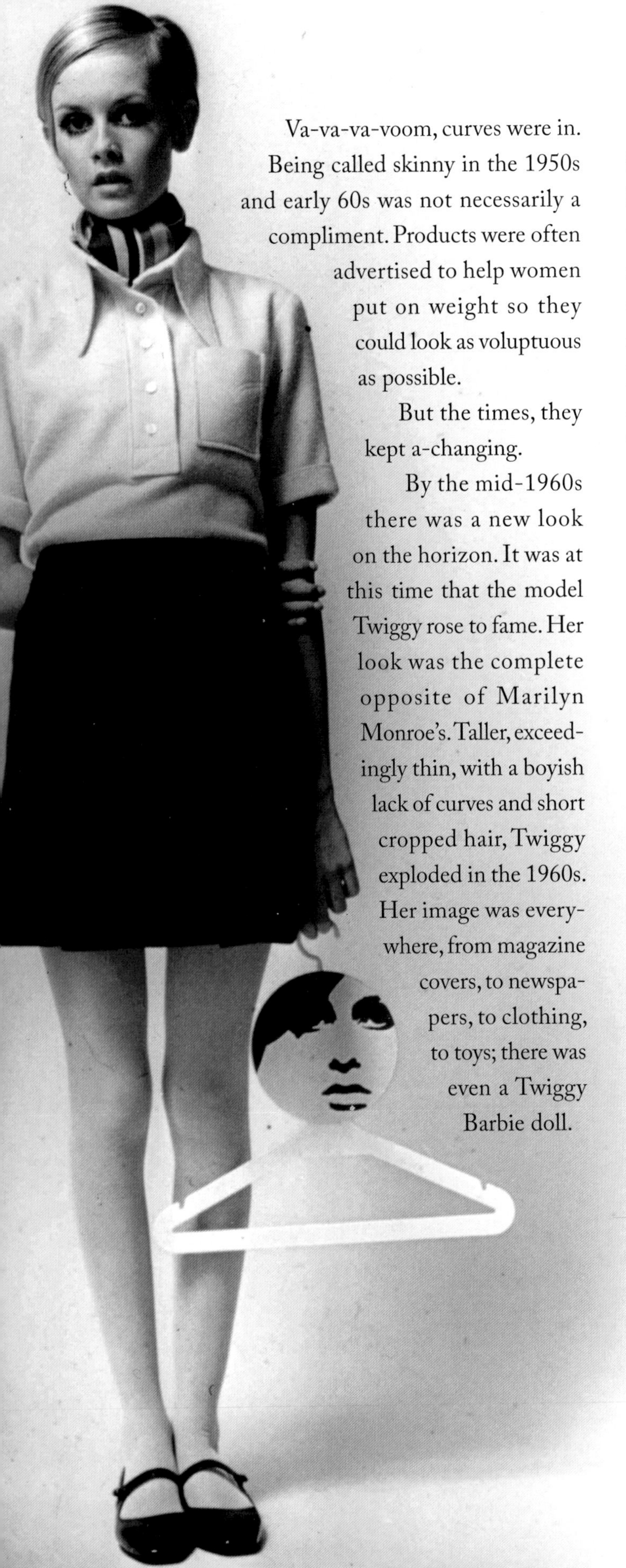

Va-va-va-voom, curves were in. Being called skinny in the 1950s and early 60s was not necessarily a compliment. Products were often advertised to help women put on weight so they could look as voluptuous as possible.

But the times, they kept a-changing.

By the mid-1960s there was a new look on the horizon. It was at this time that the model Twiggy rose to fame. Her look was the complete opposite of Marilyn Monroe's. Taller, exceedingly thin, with a boyish lack of curves and short cropped hair, Twiggy exploded in the 1960s. Her image was everywhere, from magazine covers, to newspapers, to clothing, to toys; there was even a Twiggy Barbie doll.

Unfortunately, Marilyn Monroe died tragically in 1962. But what if she had lived? How would she have been viewed in the face of changing beauty trends? Would a woman considered among the most beautiful on earth all of a sudden been viewed as unattractive? And why? Just because select fashion magazines had decided it was time for a new look? They could have picked one of a thousand different looks, but thin was the one they picked. Twiggy became the super-model of the era.

Understand that this is not about whether Marilyn or Twiggy were beautiful. They were/are both beautiful. They are just different. The problem is, as often happens, different images are not presented as being equally beautiful. **An ideal type is highlighted and then we are flooded with that image as the one and only.** When Twiggy-mania exploded, what girl stood a chance? What girl wasn't expected to compare herself to this new image of beauty? Thin was in! The problem was most girls were not built like Twiggy who was naturally — that's *naturally* — thin.

This is no different than what girls have faced for thousands of years, trying to conform to an ideal, wishing to be curvier, straighter, plumper, thinner, tanned, pale, taller, shorter — an endless and ever-changing list.

And the list changes not only according to time, but also to place.

ACROSS OCEANS

There are many cultures throughout the world that have often held very different opinions than our Western one of what is beautiful.

Mauritania

The grass is not always greener on the other side. Like many countries, Mauritania is a country in flux when it comes to the debate over ideal female body weight. But unlike North America, where many girls feel that they need to starve themselves skinny, in Mauritania the discussion is actually about how large a girl should be to be considered beautiful.

That's right. Hard as this might be for you to believe, in this West African country, the fatter the girl, the more attractive she is considered by many. Skinny girls are often pitied, and "among women, rolling layers of fat are the height of sexiness."[1] Even the stretch marks often produced through weight gain is considered sexy. In order to achieve and maintain their weight goals, some girls eat roughly ten times the calories that we consider healthy in North America.

But before you hop a plane for Mauritania with visions of ice-cream sundaes dancing in your head,

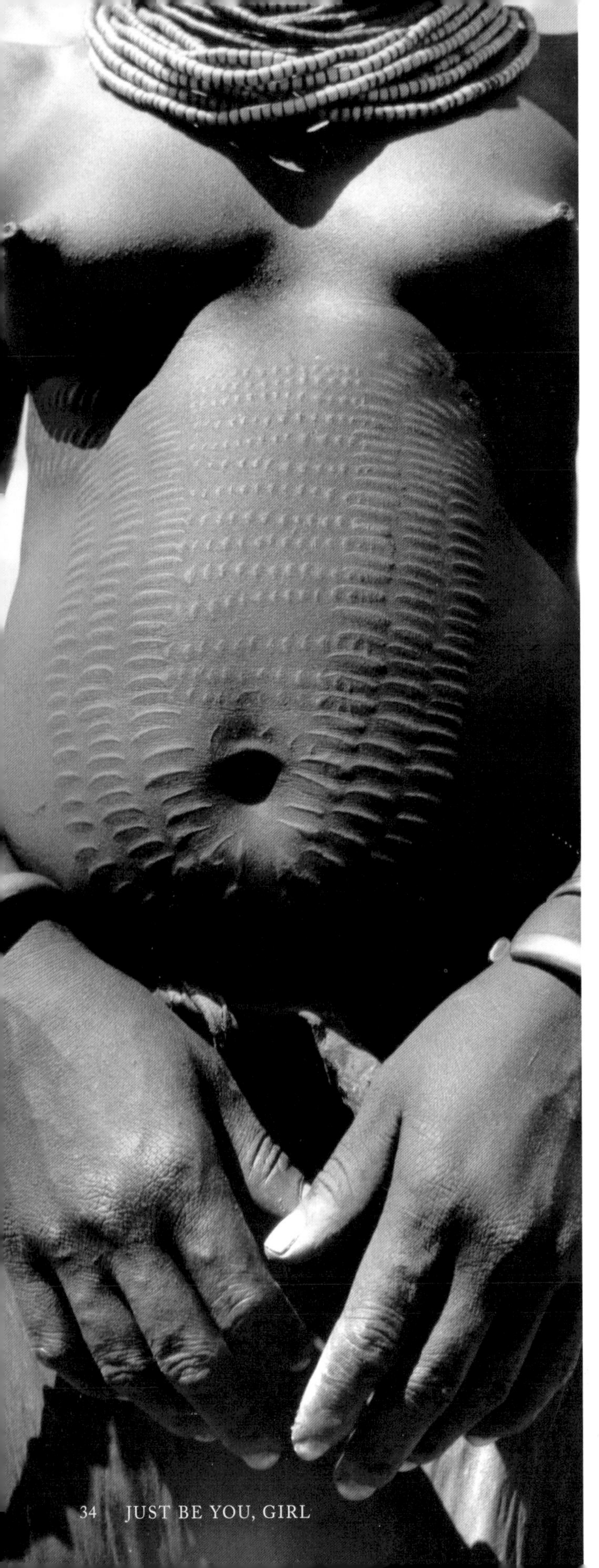

consider this. In a whacky twist of fate, girls in Mauritania are faced with exactly the same problems many girls in Western countries face. While girls in our culture may starve themselves to the point of illness, forced to live up to their ideal of beauty, girls in Mauritania often eat to the point of becoming morbidly obese and extremely unhealthy. We down the diet pills, while these girls take hormone fattening drugs to add to their weight. And just like here, the girls themselves are not the ones defining the beauty ideals, but they sure are the ones forced to live up to them.

While some girls are now standing up against these dangerous ideals, "up to one third of the country's women are still risking their lives to put on weight to conform to a long-standing aesthetic standard that has long valued big as beautiful."[2]

Karo Tribe of Ethiopia

While here we fret over the tiniest scar or blemish that appears on our body, and companies have earned millions of dollars selling creams and ointments that promise to make our skin as smooth as silk, such skin is not what is admired everywhere.

The Karo, a small tribe with an estimated population of between 1,000 and 3,000 people, live on the banks of the Omo River in southwestern Ethiopia.

Karo women scar their chests to make themselves look more beautiful. They cut their skin with a knife and rub ash into the wounds to produce a raised welt. Such scars are meant to demonstrate their strength and resistance to disease.[3]

Karo woman showing beautiful scarred chest.

Maori

Although I am sure you have seen lots of tattoos in your life, you've probably seen none like those that have adorned the women of the Maori culture of New Zealand for hundreds of years.

Ta moko is the art of Maori tattooing. This is the permanent marking of skin by carving it with chisels. In the past, a moko was used as a symbol of ones' identity. A woman's moko (tattoo) was most often marked on her chin and lips.

It was considered the height of beauty to have full blue lips.

The art of ta moko continued throughout the 20th Century. Although it then declined in frequency, there has been a resurgence of interest in the moko in recent years and there are still women who wear a moko today.[4]

Chinese Foot-binding

Although no longer practiced today, the Chinese custom of foot-binding is a cultural example of a beauty ideal that every young girl should know about.

Dating back over 1000 years, this custom began with the notion that girls with unnaturally small feet were more desirable. To ensure that their daughters would be considered beautiful and therefore marry well, mothers would bind their daughters' feet to keep them from growing.

Starting as young as age three, a girl would have her toes bent back under towards the sole of her feet until they broke. Then the feet would be bent in line with the leg so that the arch of

her foot would break. Finally the entire foot would be tightly wrapped in bandages to squish everything in and keep the foot from growing. The foot would be wrapped and tightly rebound often. The desire was that the foot would grow no larger than about 3-4 inches.

As you can imagine, this was an extremely painful process for the girl to endure. Ingrown toenails often resulted in infections. The skin around the feet would die and have to be scraped off and sometimes the toes would even fall off (this would be considered okay as it would make the foot even smaller). The foot would be so physically deformed that girls would never show them but rather only display their feet in their little slippers. Because of this deformity, it was nearly impossible for the girls to walk. All this pain and suffering was inflicted to make these girls more desirable to men and therefore better able to marry well.[5]

It might be hard for you to imagine going to such lengths to make yourself desirable to others, but remember, many of these girls had no choice. The

Adult shoes of female with bound feet beside modern baby socks.

choice was taken out of their hands by their parents. Today, girls have a choice. But what will be said a thousand years from now about girls who starve themselves until their skeletons show, making their bodies sick and weak because that is what society is telling them is desirable?

The point is that there are many different examples of how external beauty is defined, depending on when and where you live. So ultimately you have to ask yourself, what is true beauty? How can beauty ever be defined by one narrow set of external attributes?

Beauty is in the eye of the beholder, so make it your eye that counts when looking in the mirror. Don't try to change to fit popular ideals, because they are often based on factors out of your control and forever changing. Don't let a passing popular opinion dictate how you feel about yourself.

You are true beauty, because beauty is in the eye of the beholder and always has been.

Beauty: *A quality that gives pleasure to the senses.*

Sense: *Any of the faculties of perceiving things by touching, hearing, seeing, smelling or tasting.*[6]

As defined by the dictionary, people find beauty in whatever gives them pleasure and pleasure can flow not only from what one sees, but also what one feels or hears.

In this way, you can impart your beauty on the world in many other ways than just your physical appearance. There is the beauty of your heart when you use your voice to soothe a friend in times of trouble or the beauty of your spirit when your sense of humor leaves those around you feeling exhausted from laughter.

People can be attracted to you based on so many of your different qualities. If you limit yourself by obsessing about just one quality, like your physical appearance, you may actually be limiting the beauty that others will see in you.

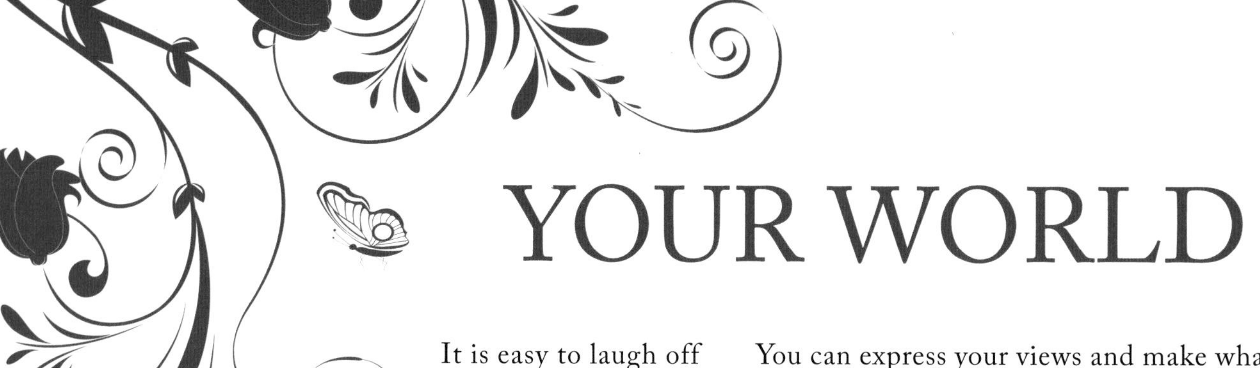

YOUR WORLD

It is easy to laugh off Elizabethan women as foolish for putting deadly lead powder on their faces just to fit in, but are today's girls, born hundreds of years later, really any more informed and independent when it comes to making healthy, individual decisions?

Sure Elizabethan ladies did not have MTV or Facebook to contend with. They didn't have to stand in line at a supermarket faced with bulging racks of beauty magazines, but they did have their own pressures. If the Royal Court decreed pale skin was in, you would do wise not to insult the Queen by ignoring her taste in fashion. If religious leaders determined that women who showed their ankles were of poor character, then you best hide your ankles if you wanted to find a suitable husband. In other words, there could be real consequences for not following the popular code of the time.

Some young girls today still face religious and cultural demands that may dictate the choices they can make in life. But, many girls in Western culture today enjoy much more freedom over their lives than girls of even just a few generations ago. You grow up today with opportunities unheard of for your grandmothers, for instance. You can choose the jobs you want, even start your own business. You can travel the world. You can run for politics. You can express your views and make whatever imprint on the world you choose. You have independence and freedom of choice unheard of less than a century ago.

If you have all this freedom and power, then why are so many tears still wasted on trying to measure up to society's image of what you should be? Why is it so hard to be happy with just who you are?

One reason is that people are complicated. Young and old, we all want our independence and freedom, but we also want to "fit in." Being part of the group offers security; it's safe not to stand out too much. There is nothing to feel ashamed about with wanting to fit in. It's perfectly natural. But when you completely give yourself over in order to fit in with a popular ideal, you can start to lose your own identity and can become depressed and anxious. You need to find the balance that is right for you — the balance that lets you explore the opportunities around you without becoming lost under their influence.

A good way to help you find your balance is to start paying more attention to the world around you. The more educated you are, the less likely you are to put yourself in harm's way, either physically or mentally, by trying to squeeze yourself into an idealized concept of perfection. The more you listen to the voice inside you instead of only reacting to popular opinion, the more likely you are to make choices that feel right for you. The more you pay attention to the world around you, the more you can stand apart from it and just be yourself.

Many of the influences in your life might seem obvious to you, or perhaps not. In either case, it never hurts to stop and take stock of the forces you encounter each day.

To be nobody but yourself in a
world which is doing its best,
night and day, to make you
everybody else means to fight
the hardest battle which any
human being can fight;
and never stop fighting.

— e.e. cummings

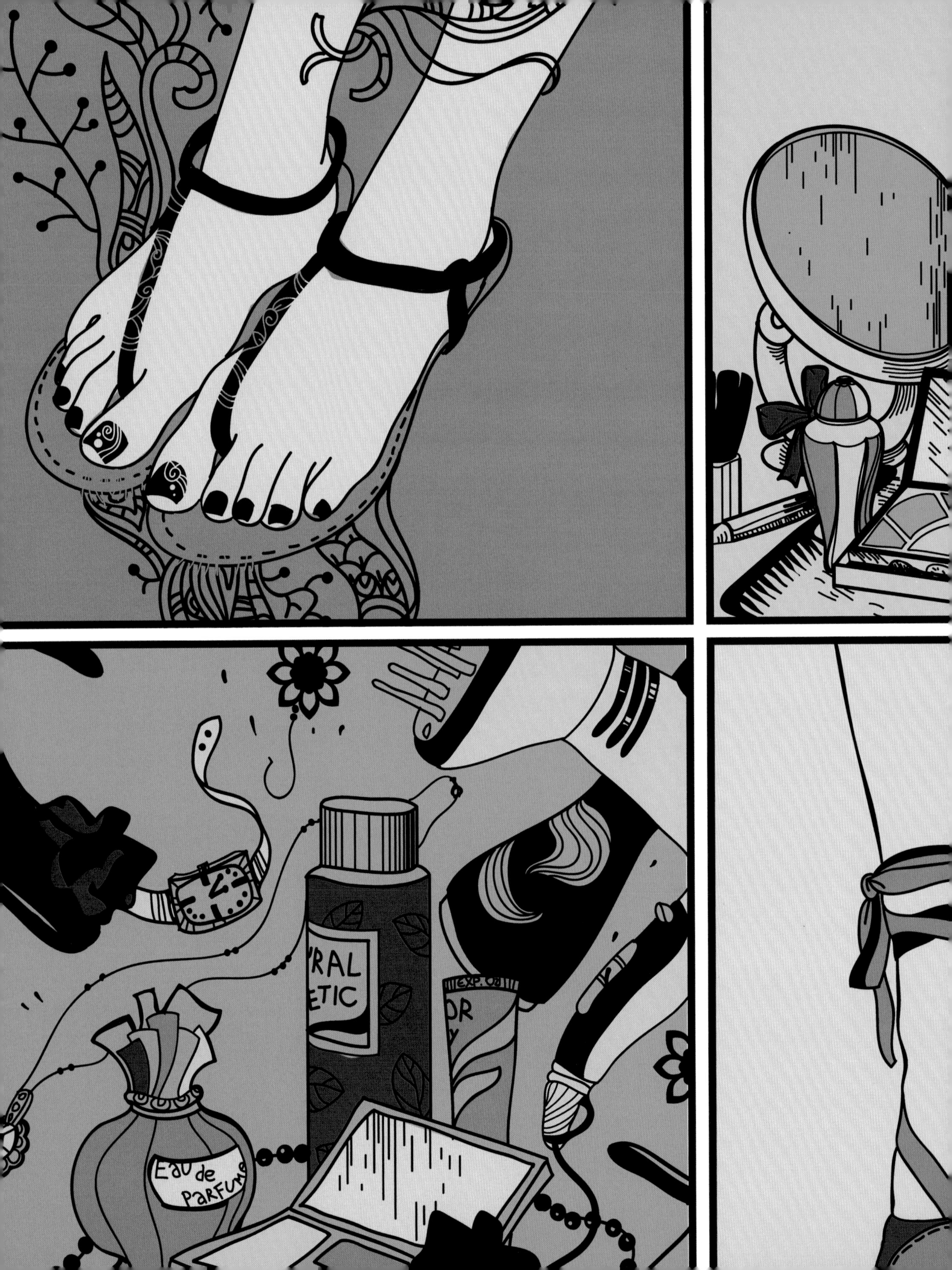
Eau de
parfume

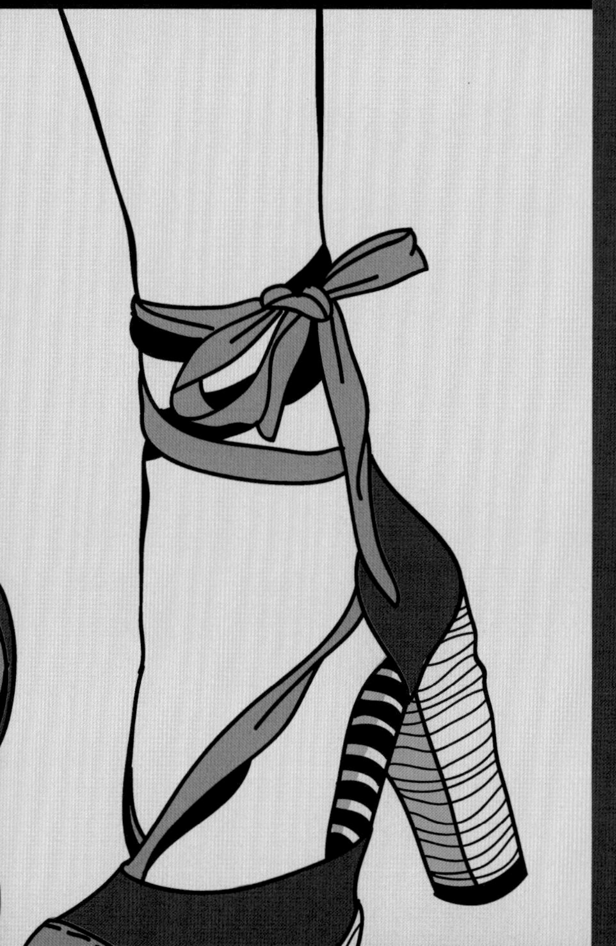

MARKETING MADNESS

What is a size 00 anyway? I'm sure many of you have asked yourself this question when looking through the racks of your favorite clothing store. It stretched the imagination when clothing manufacturers started producing size 0 clothes — I mean zero basically means nothing, so size 0, I guess, is size nothing. Who can be size nothing? But size 00? There is no value for 00 in math. There is 0 and then there is anything above 0 or there is anything less than 0, but what is 00? In clothing, would this mean you were a size nothing nothing? What the heck does that even mean?

Some say that size 0 clothing options started as a way for clothing manufacturers to make women feel better about their size. Given the pressures on us to be as thin as possible, we have become obsessed about the number on our tags. The smaller the tag size, the better we feel. So, to help us along and keep us buying, some manufacturers have simply done a switch-a-roo. Known as "vanity sizing," pants that years ago would have been size 12 may now be marked as a size 8. This means that pants that back then would have measured a size 8 are now tagged as a size 4, and so on and so on. In other words, your generation didn't suddenly produce a huge number of size 0 girls — the pant tags just make it look that way.

Compounding the problem is the fact that sizing can be very different depending on where you shop. You might be a perfect size 6 in one store, but be a size 8 in another store or even a size 10 in a third store. You haven't changed sizes between stores, but your self-esteem has probably plunged as you moved from the first store to the third store.

The point is that **this is just one example of how many of the things we believe to be true are really just illusions.** The size you see on the tag of your jeans isn't real; it shifts and changes depending on when and where you buy them. If you desperately want to fit into a smaller size of jeans, just for the sake of seeing that smaller number on the tag, then perhaps instead of starving yourself to the point of illness, all you really need to do is find a different store where the jeans are sized differently. Or better yet, decide for yourself what makes you look and feel good. Don't be controlled by made-up guidelines and labels.

According to a study done by Dr. Tammy Kinley of the University of North Texas, pant sizing can vary greatly depending on where you shop. In her study, Dr. Kinley measured 1,000 pair of size 4 pants and found as much as an 8-inch difference in the waist size!

THE SECRETS OF SELLING

***Marketing is the total of activities involved in the transfer of goods from the producer or seller to the consumer or buyer, including advertising, shipping, storing and selling.*[1]**

I know this looks an awful lot like something you would see in a textbook. Ugh! But there is not going to be a test on this later. It is just that if you want to understand all the invisible forces that influence your daily decisions and the way you feel about yourself, you really, really, really (three reallys = very important) need to understand what marketing is (but you don't have to memorize the definition).

A lot of times people use the word marketing and advertising to mean the same thing; this is sort of true, but not exactly. Advertising is a direct message aimed at telling you something. All those slick commercials you see on television telling you that "if you buy this shampoo your hair will shine to the point of glowing in the dark"— that's advertising. The beautiful pictures you see in the magazines with the impossibly perfect girl lovingly looking at her sparkling new bracelet, as though now that she owns this object the world is complete — that's advertising. It is a direct message aimed at making you believe something specific about a product or service. Advertising tells you directly that if you buy what they are selling you will be better in some way.

Marketing, on the other hand, can be a little more subtle, meaning that you might not even realize that you are being directed to want a certain product or service. While marketing can include the use of advertising, it can also use other means to influence your decisions. It can include things like pricing, store design, special events, contests, sponsorships, and any number of things that will let you know either directly or indirectly that you should buy what they have to sell and that if you do buy *it*, you will be much better than before you had *it*.

For example, many fashion companies will give their product to certain people free of charge, like an up-and-coming actress, just to get her to wear it. If your favorite television star is suddenly wearing pink polka-dotted furry boots, guess what you are all of a sudden not going to be able to live without? No one told you that you had to buy them, they just subtly suggested that it is the "cool" thing to have on.

Another example is that some stores play music so loud that it discourages older people from wanting to be in the store. So instead of going into the store with their daughters, mothers simply send the girls in with the cash while they wait next door in the nice quiet coffee shop. Stores know that it is easier to influence a young girl into purchasing something if the sales staff does not have to get past the mother as well.

Sales staff in stores can be very intimidating, not just to young girls, but to everyone, men and women of all ages. They are trained to sell things — that is their job. The more they sell to you, the better they are doing their job. This isn't to say that salespeople are dishonest or bad in any way. They just have a job to do, and you need to understand that.

How often has a sales clerk asked you if you can really afford that purchase you are going to make? Have you ever been stopped at the check-out and asked how practical those fur-lined, studded stilettos are in your everyday life? Or have you ever been told that the pants you are about to buy are wickedly overpriced in this store, but can be found cheaper at another? Have you ever been told that the dress you are about to buy looks horrible on you? Probably not very often, if ever.

However, I'm guessing you probably have heard that you look "super cute in that jacket" or that "those pants are in the must-have color of the season" or that the sweater you are purchasing is their "absolute favorite."

Stores are a magical place. They make you feel smart and beautiful for buying what they have to sell. That is their job. It is your job to understand this and to make your own decisions about what you want and can afford. If you want to wear fur-lined, studded stilettos then go for it, but know that before you enter the store or you might be shaking your head the next day when you open up the shoe

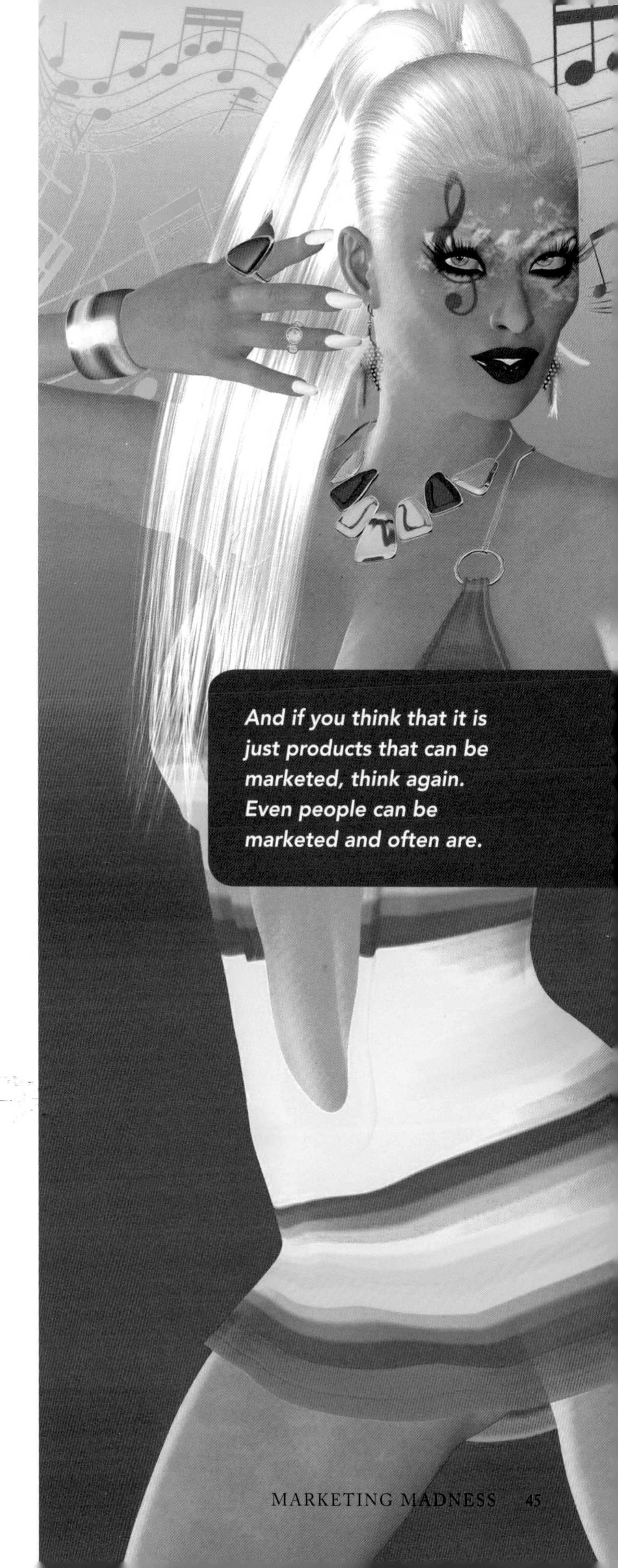

And if you think that it is just products that can be marketed, think again. Even people can be marketed and often are.

box wondering how exactly you were convinced that these were a good purchase!

And if you think that it is just products that can be marketed, think again. Anything and everything can be marketed (including this book you are reading). Even people can be marketed and often are.

When you try to be exactly like that famous singer from MTV, understand that you can't really be like her because you really know nothing about her. You are copying the *image* that she projects. She gets paid to look and sound and be the way she is. It is part of her image. It is part of her job.

The outrageous clothes she wears are costumes, meant to entertain you. If she wears 5-inch heels and dances around in an itty-bitty miniskirt, it is part of an act. She is marketing herself so that she can sell you something (her music or perfume or whatever). She is saying, "Look at me, look at how sexy I am, look at how much fun I am having. If you want to be like me, then dress like me, buy my music or perfume or clothes or whatever."

But what you don't see is the back story. You only see what they want you to see. If you want to be like her because she is a singer, then buying her perfume will not make you a singer. Years of focus, hard work and music training will help you.

If you are dressing like her because her life looks so fantastically fun, then consider these points. First, you know nothing about her real life. You know the pictures you are shown where she is always dancing and laughing in fantastic clothes next to really cute guys. That is called publicity — only show what you want seen. In reality, you know nothing about her daily schedule, financial situation, love life or stress level. Perhaps she is fantastically happy *or* perhaps she is overstressed, addicted to drugs and that cute guy she is pictured with is actually a real jerk who treats her like dirt. The point is you don't really know.

Second, how is copying her image or buying her stuff going to make you like her? You will still be you only in 5-inch heels and an itty-bitty miniskirt. You will not suddenly be famous and carefree because the person you are copying is not carefree. She has a job. She is a singer, which required a lot of focus, confidence, hard work and training, not just cool clothes.

The thing is, if you like the smell of her perfume, it makes sense to buy it. If you really like the style of clothes she wears and feel good wearing 5-inch heels and itty-bitty miniskirts, then that is your choice (although your folks might have something to say about that). But if you are doing these things in the hopes of having all the promised dreams of another person, then understand that the person you are trying to copy might just be an illusion, just like the tag size on your pants.

IMAGINE

Consider some of the things you want in life. Not right now (like I want those new boots), but overall in your life.

Pretend you are very, very old and sadly coming to the end of your life. Now envision yourself looking back on your life and recounting to your great grandchildren what your life was like. What would you like to be able to tell them about who you were and what you did? Would you hope to say something like?

- I was a writer.
- I saw the world.
- I was loved and happy.
- I had a farm with lots of horses.
- I had my own business.

Or, can you envision saying something like?

- I was a size 00.
- My hair always looked perfect.
- I only ever wore the latest fashions.
- I spent hours worrying about what others thought of me and how I looked.
- I never did go for my dream because I always felt that I was not good enough.

Why is this important?

You may think this is a silly exercise. It is not meant to make you feel stupid for wanting to look good or buy the latest fashions. It is sometimes only when we put things down in black and white that we realize that we can lose sight of the forest for the trees or, in other words, lose sight of the overall opportunities in life when we focus only on the immediate concerns.

Sure, every girl wants perfect hair, and there is nothing wrong with wanting to make yourself look a certain way, but you need to remember that unless these things are your end goal in life, most of them will not contribute to what is really going to satisfy you in the long run. No one cares how tall or short their doctor is, you can still be a writer despite your pimples and there is no perfect look that will guarantee you love and happiness no matter how many advertisers tell you differently.

YOU'RE WORTH A BILLION

Businesses love you. Young women control billions of consumer dollars. I know that you are thinking, "I have like $20 to my name. How can I be so important?" But consider how much money you have spent in the last year on clothes, cosmetics, books, movies, music, etc. You might not have spent all the money yourself, but it is not just how much of your own money you have spent, it is also how much was spent on you by parents, grandparents, aunts and uncles, friends and so on. All of the purchases these people made for you were based on what you like.

So you not only control the money you spend directly, but also the money that a lot of other people spend. Multiply this by all the young girls out there, and you begin to realize that, as a group, you and your friends and countless other young girls control a lot of spending. This is why businesses love you. They all want to get a piece of all that money that is being spent.

The problem is that you can spend your money in so many different ways. You can spend it on books instead of clothes, or on candy instead of movies or you could decide to save your money and not spend it at all. Even if you do decide to buy, let's say some perfume, well, you could have dozens or hundreds of perfumes to choose from. How is a company going to get you to buy their perfume?

Companies have three problems. First, you have to decide that you want to buy the product they sell. Second, you have to decide that you want to buy their product and not one of their competitors'. Third, they want to ensure that you buy as much of that product as possible. Why buy one pair of jeans, when you could own 24? This is why businesses spend so much time and money marketing to you. You would not believe how much power you have over business!

Disclaimer

I really want to stop here and say that the purpose of this section is to help you to understand how marketing can influence how you feel about yourself if you are not aware of how it works. It is in no way to say that all advertisers/marketers are bad and are out to trick you. There are a lot of great things we have in our lives thanks to the companies that produce them. Amazing and helpful products are created every day that enrich our lives. Marketing these products helps us to learn about them, which is great.

However, and this is a big however, there is also a ton of consumer waste on our planet. Landfills filled with things that we no longer want and probably never needed. People of all ages go into financial debt daily by spending on things that they simply can't afford. And perhaps just as sad is the fact that many of us can be left feeling less adequate

and somehow lacking when we don't seem to achieve the effects that are promised by some of the products that are marketed to us. We are often convinced that a product or service can somehow completely remake us and our lives, and that, in fact, our lives need to be improved (advertising rarely implies that you are good just the way you are).

Marketing can sometimes overreach and promise things, directly or indirectly, that the product cannot fulfill. This can leave us angry, confused and more than a few pennies short in our bank account, but only if we don't know how it works. If you understand the purpose of marketing and some of the tricks of the trade, then hopefully you are in a better position to decipher the images and messages around you so that you do not get lost in them or overwhelmed by them. You need to take control and determine which messages actually benefit you and which are merely using you for their own end. You are young, but you are smart — educate yourself, know yourself and trust yourself.

You need to take control and determine which messages actually benefit you and which are merely using you for their own end.

ADVERTISING TRICKS

There are lots of ways to sell a product, but let's deal with the most obvious — advertising.

Advertising is the most blatant form of selling. Advertising doesn't try to hide what it is doing; it screams at you from billboards, bus shelters, television, radio, magazines and pretty much any other place you can stick a message, including all over the Internet on sites like YouTube and Facebook.

Advertising is intimidating. It is meant to be. The sole purpose of advertising is to tell you that you need to buy the product it's selling and that, if you do, your life will be better. Often not said, but completely implied, is the opposite. If you do not buy what they are selling you will somehow be less than everyone who does buy the product; you will be left out of the *cool* crowd.

You might think that advertising doesn't affect you. And maybe one or two or ten messages would not. But thousands of messages constantly bombarding you wear you down, even if you don't know it. If you see hundreds of messages every day with a perfect looking model staring out at you, how could you not begin to feel inadequate? Who wouldn't start to stare at themselves a little longer in the mirror and begin to compare? You are not alone. You would be hard pressed to find any girl (or woman) who does not somehow feel inadequate when faced with these countless images of perfection.

There are lots of tricks to advertising effectively. You don't need to become a specialist in advertising, but it is good to get a sense of some of the methods advertisers use in order to better understand how advertising can affect, not only the choices you make, but how you feel about yourself. **The better you understand the things around you, the better you can control how they make you feel**. So here are just a couple of the tricks you may want to be aware of.

The Bombardment

Advertisers will overwhelm you by constantly bombarding you with their message. If you can't escape the message, then eventually you begin to believe it. When faced with the exact same image of beauty over and over, you begin to think, "Oh, that is what I should look like." Or, another example is the *seasonal trend*, as in, "The trend for this season is polka-dotted sunglasses; the hot color this season is fuchsia; the must-have items this summer are skinny jeans and furry boots."

Now, you might never have thought you needed polka-dotted sunglasses, you might not even look good in skinny jeans, but after the thousandth time that you are told that all the cool kids have furry boots, then you have to be pretty strong willed not to also want some furry boots (preferably in fuchsia).

Understand where your decisions are coming from. Why do you unexpectedly need fuchsia furry boots? Do you put them on and go, “Thank goodness, where have you been all my life? I look fantastic.” Or do you say, “These are so comfortable and warm, they are just what I needed.” If yes, then great. You have been introduced to a product through advertising that you really like and offers you a benefit.

Or do you just buy them, like a robot, because you are convinced by all of the messages that you need them regardless of how they look on you, feel on you, fit your activities or your budget. Just blindly following a fashion trend can actually make you feel worse about yourself. Sure, you may “fit in” because you are wearing what everyone else is wearing, but maybe the look isn’t flattering to you and doesn’t

A lot of girls in my class wear mismatched socks. You might think that we do this because we want to follow the trend some new singer or actress started or that we want to be a little bit different. But guess what? Neither of those are the reasons!

I started doing this in grade four or five. It was because I couldn't find any clean socks that matched in my drawer. I had to wear something so I just picked a couple of socks and put them on. I figured that no one would notice — because who sees socks? They are covered by boots or shoes! If anyone did notice, it didn't bother me. My socks are clean and my feet are happy!

Now, I do try to wear two ankle socks or two long socks, but they definitely don't have to match. Today I have on one monkey ankle sock and one striped ankle sock. The weird thing is that lots of other girls in my class do the same thing, for some reason. We didn't all decide one day to start wearing mismatched socks, it just sort of happened. "Or," as my brother would say, "did it?"

— G

fit your body type or your personality, so now you actually feel worse about yourself because when you look in the mirror you don't like the way you look or feel. Clothes should enhance how you feel about yourself; if they don't then there is something wrong with the choice. Better to be daring and stand apart from the crowd in outfits that you know you feel good in.

Once you pause to think about where your desires are coming from, you can sort through them and the decisions you make because of them. Be your own leader. The sad truth is that no matter how popular some fashions are, some things may just not work for you. That's okay; we are all different. The important thing is to find the style that fits not only your body type, but who you are as a person (those super cute high heel boots are probably not going to be the most practical for playing in the snow). When you trust and honor your own judgment you are more likely to make choices that will truly make you feel good about yourself.

Creating and Using Your Insecurities

This may sound harsh (sorry), but some advertisers count on the fact that young girls — you — are self-absorbed and can easily be made to feel insecure (don't feel bad, they count on most people having these qualities). Together these two factors make it easier for an advertiser to plant a seed of doubt in your mind that perhaps you are not quite all that you should be. If you can be convinced of an imagined problem, then it is easier to sell you the solution.

Two of the easiest ways to make a young girl feel insecure is to focus on her looks and her social standing, in other words, your beauty and your popularity. Who does not want beauty and popularity? So, it would follow that the easiest way to sell to you is to imply that you are not yet quite beautiful or popular enough and then sell you a solution.

The tragedy of this technique is that in order to get you to the point of buying, you are often made to feel a little bad about yourself first.

There are lots of obvious ads that play on your desire to be more beautiful, and we'll talk about this later, when the use of models is discussed, but many ads play on these insecurities a little more subtly. They want to capitalize on your insecurities, but not directly. No advertiser wants to come right out and insult you. So it is merely implied.

Take, for instance, the common cell phone commercial targeting young girls. It runs something like this: *a group of very put together young girls is dancing and laughing together in the school hall or maybe a sleepover shot where they are all goofing around and snapping pics of one another and then texting those pics to each other, then cue the cute boys somewhere in the commercial — maybe they call the girls on their phones.* The point is, all the girls in the commercial have the same generic good looks and are having a lot of fun with all their friends (popular). The implied message is that if your life doesn't look like this every day then there is something wrong, but no problem, because if you have this cell phone you will instantly be invited to the party.

BUSINESS
LOADING 100%
WORLD
-ASIA
-AFRICA
NETWORK
-VIDEO
-MUSIC
-FILMS
-SEARCH

When you see an example like this in black and white, it might look obvious to the point of lame. You may even feel insulted by the suggestion that you would fall for such a blatant message. But don't sell advertisers short. This type of messaging is proven to work time and time again (and not just with young girls). Remember, people innately want to fit in. When seeing it on paper, it may be obvious to you that merely buying a cell phone will not launch you to instant popularity, but when combined with the bombardment of this message, you will begin to feel that this device does hold the magical key to happiness.

And herein lies the danger. You have left reason at the door — twice! First, you have allowed yourself to believe that unless you are dancing down the halls of your school with perfect perkiness you are missing out and, second, that this particular product will instantly teleport you to this new life. Stop and think — no one's life is like it is portrayed on commercials no matter what product they buy. You know this already. When was the last time you saw someone spontaneously break out into song and dance on the street? Maybe it would be nice if this happened more often, but it is unlikely to any time soon.

So concentrate on all the good things in your life right now. If you feel that you would like things to be different then decide on some realistic goals and how to attain them. **Dealing with reality is a much quicker way to obtain what you want than hoping that some magical product will deliver it.**

TRICK

Overpromising

We all fall for this, regardless of how old we are. The hope is that as we get a little older, we fall for this a little less (or at least with our eyes wide open).

There are a lot of good products out there that do what they say they will do. Products that can help with dry skin, or hairy legs or pimples. Not all products might work for you, though this doesn't mean the product is purposely overpromising what it can do. For example, skin types are different. Sometimes a product that can help clear pimples might work for your friend and not for you. So you may have to use some trial and error to find the things that work best for you and your specific needs.

However, throughout the ages there has been no shortage of advertisements that promise everything from the unprovable to the impossible — promises of products that will make you thinner, taller, smarter or happier with just a little dab of ointment or pop of a pill. These were not products hawked in back allies, but rather advertised in trusted beauty magazines and publications

You might think that such outlandish ads are a thing of the past — but you would be wrong. Fantastic claims are being made all the time by products, even today. Although, with people's increased understanding of how the body works (and the ability to sue manufacturers for false claims), the

Vintage Advertising

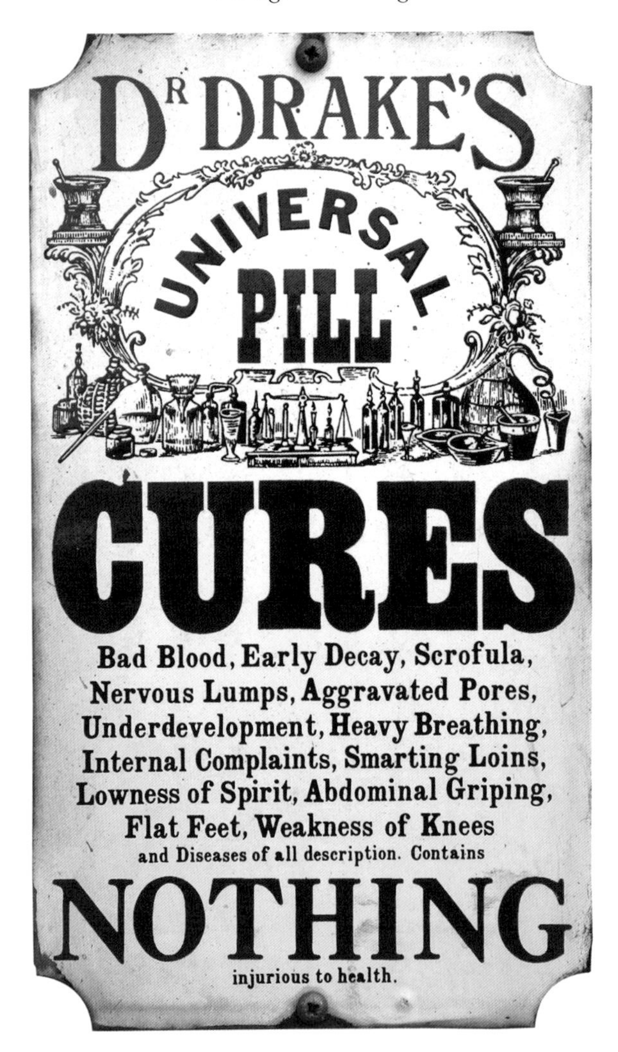

most outrageous of these products are usually now contained to the mystical world of Internet pop-ups. So while these ads may still exist today, they are not really the problem. Hopefully, you have all stayed awake long enough in health class to realize that you can't wash away fat or cure everything with just one pill.

The more deceitful of the ads today, and the ones that can really affect how you feel about yourself, are much more subtle in their claims. And they can leave you feeling unhappy with yourself for two main reasons.

First, they bombard you with an image that they portray as ideal — an image that might not match what you see in the mirror. So now you have been told you have a problem. That you need to be fixed. Second, they offer you a solution that (if not stated outright) clearly implies that your problem can be fixed by their product. **So if you don't get the results promised by the ad, then you are left to feel like a failure.**

The reality is, Mother Nature blessed you with certain attributes — some you may love, some you may not be too fond of; some you may be able to change, but some you may just have to live with. The truth is, what Mother Nature decides cannot always be changed by a store-bought elixir, no matter what the commercial says. So once all is said and done, you may be left feeling that you don't measure up to the ideal presented in the commercial and that even this product, which clearly makes the models on the commercial perfect, can't fix you.

Shampoo commercials are a good example of this. Shampoo commercials promise the world. They continually show girls with incredibly long, overly thick, blindingly shiny hair twirling around with nary a strand out of place. The message usually runs something like this, *"For stronger, thicker hair in only weeks, use Shampoo X.*" The reality is different. While such shampoos can clean your hair, and nourish them, even reduce hair breakage, no shampoo is going to be able to deliver triple thick hair to someone who has naturally thin hair. (I know this!) Mother Nature wins.

So how do ads get away with this you may ask? Well, it is because they are so subtle in their message. They don't say that your hair will grow x inches thicker. They merely say that it will be stronger, thicker, healthier, etc. Who has the time, money or actual knowledge to prove that your hair isn't somehow healthier by using this shampoo? It's not what they say, it's what they show. And that is why beauty products, especially, are advertised with such stunning visuals. They show the girl with Rapunzel hair, but they don't actually tell you that their product made her hair that way because Mother Nature had already done it (assuming that it is actually not faked with wigs, hair extensions or video tricks).

If they are forced to make an actual concrete claim in order to sell the product, then look for the fine print! Diet ads are famous for their fine print. First they show these stunning before and after photos that make the weight loss look like it's one pill or drink supplement away. But if you look really close, like with one of those space telescopes that NASA uses, you often see (maybe) all of this teeny tiny print on the bottom of the screen. You usually can't catch it all, but phrases like "not typical results" and "in conjunction with diet and exercise" are sure to be found.

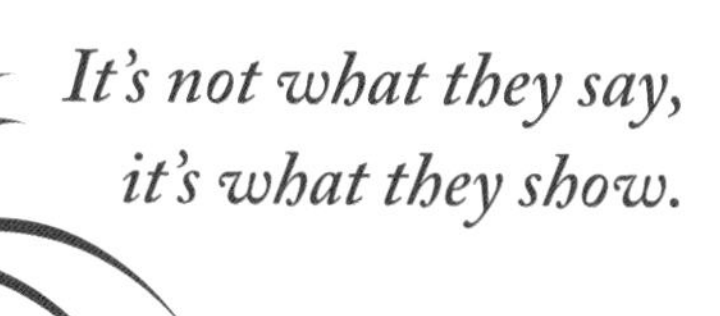

It's not what they say, it's what they show.

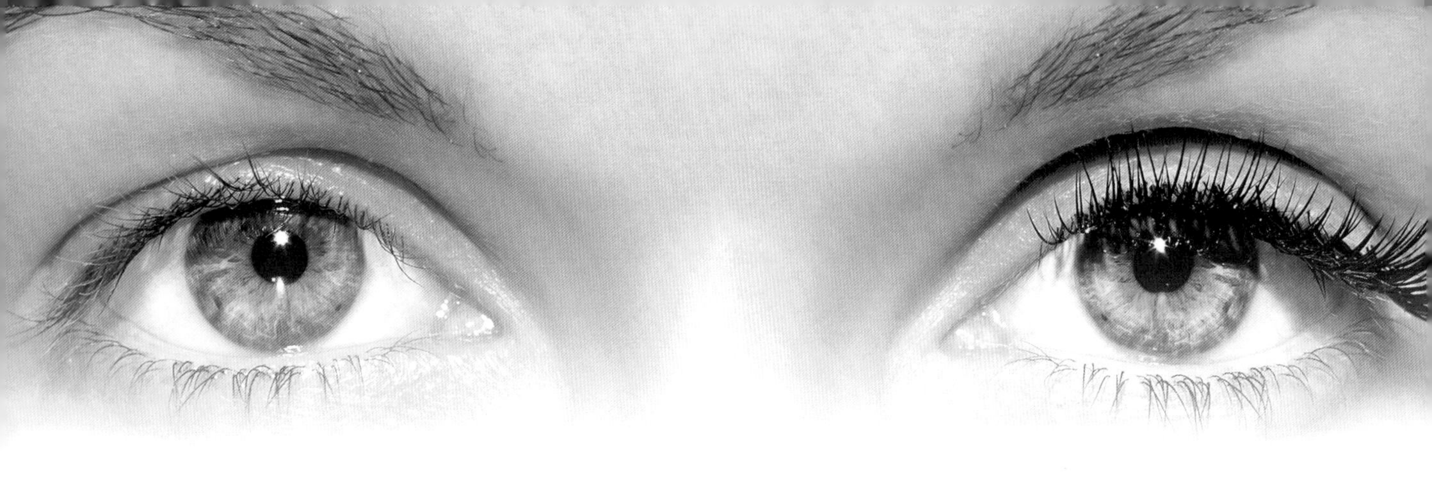

You are smart. Most times you probably already know when a product's claim is too good to be true. Always listen to your gut. If you want to try something anyway, great, just don't rely on any product to make you happy.

If you are unsure of the claims of any product, then ask around. Don't be embarrassed to ask. It can be hard to tell sometimes what is real and what is not. The Internet can be a good tool (always remember when using the Internet, the safety guidelines you have been taught at home and school). The Internet has allowed customers to easily publish their reviews of products. Remember, different things might work for different people, but reviews can offer you some good starting information. Also, knowledgeable adults are a great source of information. We have been around longer and have probably already tried what you are looking at. So save your pennies and ask before you buy.

Finally, don't get discouraged because you don't match all the images you see around you and don't try to fix or change everything about yourself to try to mirror those images. You will end up much happier if you spend your time discovering who you are and appreciating all of the great qualities (both inside and out) that you have been blessed with.

Eyelashes are a favorite for enhancement in advertisements, either through the use of false lashes or through post-production manipulation (sometimes in teeny tiny print, it will actually say on the ad that lash inserts were used but not always). However, even after being called out on such tactics, many advertisers have not stopped the practice. Remember that the next time you see those long gorgeous lashes staring out from the mascara ad. You can't always trust what you see.

The Hairy Truth

If your hair causes you grief, you are not alone. When asked, "What aspect of yourself would you most like to change?" one in four girls picked their hair.[2] This number is an average, but can rise dramatically depending on a girl's ethnic background or nationality. Regardless of your background, hair is definitely a defining characteristic of many young girls (and women).

Who has not heard the oft used excuse for being grumpy put down to "I'm having a bad hair day." Females spend billions of dollars on hair-care products and if we don't get the results we desire it can leave us devastated. After all, we have all been raised on a steady diet of Disney princesses with their long flowing tresses always perfectly blowing in the wind — a hard look to duplicate for many of us. Whether your hair is exceedingly thin, overly kinky or just out of control, many tears have been shed trying to live up to an ideal hair standard.

If you hate your hair it can be traumatic. The same way it can be traumatic if you hate your skin, your weight or any of your features. But this is what this whole book is about. Asking you to think about how much time and energy you want to devote to feeling bad about yourself over one element of who you are; and reminding you that there is more than one ideal of beauty.

If you can't achieve long, thick hair then cut it into a short pixie and rock it. If your hair is wild and kinky, then wear it proudly. Ultimately, only you can decide how much time you want to spend fretting on this subject, or how much money you want to spend trying to control it. But always remember, hair is just one more feature of who you are. It is not the only defining feature. You may not love every aspect of yourself, but know this — you were made beautiful and unique.

And P.S.: Don't get fooled by all that long, flowing hair you always see in advertising and on TV. What you are seeing is not always real.

THE MODEL

No image strikes more fear, jealousy or aspiration into the hearts of girls (be they young or old) than that of the model. A part of us hates them, while a bigger part of us wants to be them. The use of models is everywhere in advertising and really should be considered as a trick under the previous section. However, the influence of models in shaping your self-perceptions can be so strong that this topic really warrants its own discussion.

Let's be clear about one thing. If you think that this section is going to make you feel better about yourself by model-bashing, sorry, but that's not going to happen. Meanness begets meanness. In other words, you can't become happier and more confident in yourself by tearing others down. Self-esteem comes from within you. If you truly want to feel good about yourself and take charge of your life, then you need to concentrate on yourself. And, as will be repeated over and over again, educate yourself. Models are not evil creatures out to make you feel bad about yourself, but there are inherent problems within this industry that can and do affect how you feel about yourself.

Perhaps some of the blame lies with us as well. When we can't change the world around us, we need to look inside ourselves in order to control our reactions to it. This is not always easy, especially when faced with overwhelming pressures, but it can be done. You can do it. So let's take a look at both sides of the equation.

The First Side of the Equation: The Image

Let's start with the reality. Models are used everywhere in advertising, even to sell products that have nothing to do with the beauty or clothing industry. It can be incredibly hard for you to feel good about yourself when daily faced with dozens or hundreds of pictures of a female image that doesn't reflect what you see in the mirror.

So let's talk about the reality of the images you are seeing.

THEY'RE SO THIN

The first thing most girls notice about that image is how thin models are. If we were playing one of those word association games and I said the word "model," I would bet my dog that over 90% of the responses would be "thin."

And that would be true. Although exact numbers are often hard to pin down and forever shifting, the trends are unmistakable. Today, the average fashion model tends to be taller than the average woman and thinner (much thinner). Twenty years ago, fashion models weighed, on average, 8% less than the average woman. Today, the average fashion model weighs roughly 23% less than the average woman.[3] Although the argument could be made that models aren't thinner than before, in reality the average woman has just gotten heavier, many runway models today actually meet the Body Mass Index (BMI) criteria to be considered anorexic.[4]

This means that girls who could have modeled 20 years ago might no longer succeed in this industry. Are these girls suddenly not beautiful? No. It's just that now, with a culture obsessed with being shockingly thin, even *these* girls are being given the message that they don't measure up to the ideal. And maybe the girls you see model today will not measure up in twenty years from now. Although that's hard to believe because many models today are already struggling just to be thin.

Some girls are born naturally very thin. But the average body type is not "model" thin — not even for models. The news is full of stories of young models who are starving themselves to fit the model image, sometimes with tragic results. That's right, even models struggle with body image, trying to maintain the ideal.

THEY ALWAYS LOOK SO PERFECT

Yes, models are thin, but how you see them on the magazine covers, on the billboards and in the TV ads goes beyond thinness. They are seemingly perfect — porcelain, flawless skin — not a mark anywhere on their entire body. No pimples on their face, or razor

BMI, or Body Mass Index, is a commonly used tool for calculating healthy weight. It uses a person's height and weight to get an indication of body fat. Contrary to popular opinion though, BMI doesn't directly measure body fat. It also doesn't take into account muscle or bone density. So, a big boned or muscular person (an athlete for example) may have a high BMI, but not be overweight.[5]

stubble on their legs, no stray eyebrow hairs or undefined bumps — no dimpling or pimpling of any kind. Perfect hair, gleaming teeth and glowing skin. Where do they find these girls?

Well, they don't, actually. They don't exist. Yes, models are pretty, but the image of perfection that is forever staring at you from one ad or another borders on the make-believe.

Even the most beautiful girl isn't born with camera-ready looks, so photographers/advertisers help the image along, perfecting both the model's looks and the final photographs through a series of enhancements. So take heart, no one wakes up looking like they just stepped off a magazine cover. There are tons of little photography tricks that involve camera angles and lighting to bring out the best in an image, but there are also two other techniques that are widely used — stylists and airbrushing.

There are actually a lot of great videos on the Internet that show how a model (or movie star) prepares for a camera shoot. They are worth checking out in order to rebalance the reality of how a person actually looks compared to the final images you see.

Models can spend hours in the makeup chair before being photographed. They have professional stylists do their hair and makeup. Heavy makeup to cover any blemishes, bronzers to tone the skin, hair extensions to add body and length, false eyelashes for a fuller affect and dozens of other style tricks to improve on what Mother Nature gave them.

It's not just the face that gets the makeup. If there is a full body shot, there is full body makeup (remember that the next time you see those perfectly bronzed, smooth, hairless legs on a poster).

So far, so fair. At this point, there is no "cheating." Nothing is being done in the makeup chair that, technically, you couldn't do as well if you are so inclined. Just know that stylists are professionals, so for you to copy the look would take the investment of learning, time and money (makeup is not cheap!). But if this is an area that interests you and you can realistically afford the necessary tools, then great — go for it. The key point here is to understand that no one is naturally flawless and only you can decide how much of your time and money you want to spend every day trying to make yourself so. But be careful, because when you become too obsessed with one facet of your life (in this case your looks), you could be losing out on a whole lot of fun in other areas.

Unlike stylists, however, airbrushing is absolutely not playing fair. As if taking a beautiful girl and spending hours doing her hair and makeup were not enough, photographers/advertisers/magazine editors (whoever is in charge!) still say "not good enough!" and then manipulate the image using computer techniques to produce an image that not even the most beautiful, professionally styled model could match. Think about it, this is just insane. These are the images you are seeing daily; these are the images that you are comparing yourself to; these are the images that are making you feel bad about yourself. *These images are not real.*

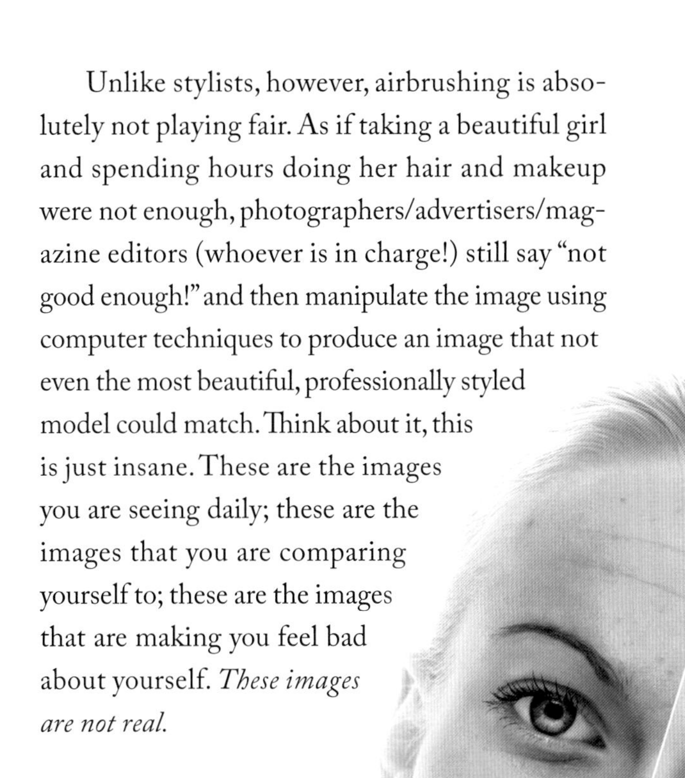

These are the images you are seeing daily; these are the images that you are comparing yourself to; these are the images that are making you feel bad about yourself. These images are not real.

Any remaining blemishes or discolorations are simply airbrushed away. Legs not long or shapely enough, a little trim here and a tuck there with the computer mouse and ta da — instant body re-do. There are even examples where a magazine put someone's head on another person's body or completely changed a particular body part and, in a few extreme cases, models' bodies have been Photoshopped to such a degree that their heads appear larger than their waists. But mostly a lot of subtle changes are made — extend the neck, lengthen the leg, smooth the hips — presto bango a whole new you.

Where Am I?

Just like many girls struggle because they don't see their body type reflected in the fashion industry, so too can it be difficult for many girls who don't see their skin color or features reflected in the countless media images that surround them.

In a 2014 annual review of New York Fashion Week, it was found that the models at the show were overwhelmingly White — nearly 80% of the runway models at this prestigious event were classified as White, about 10% as Black and only 8% as Asian. Other ethnicities barely registered.[6]

Although it is very difficult to nail down statistics across media, there is no denying what you regularly see. Overwhelmingly the North American models that adorn our runways, billboards and magazines have very Caucasian (White) characteristics.

This is just another example of why it is so important to see yourself as an important individual and not look to outside images to validate your own unique beauty or worth.

Beware the Photos You See Online

Jealous of those vacation pics your friend posted of herself looking great in that bikini? Think that guy's profile picture is really hot? Well what you are seeing might not be as real as you think because even you can retouch photos.

Photo-retouching for the average person is becoming big business. Either through do-it-yourself apps or by using the professional services of others, you too can airbrush your way to the body and face that you want. But consider this. Eventually you will have to meet people in person and introduce them to the real you. So why not work on being proud of the real you rather than spending the time learning computer generated make-believe?

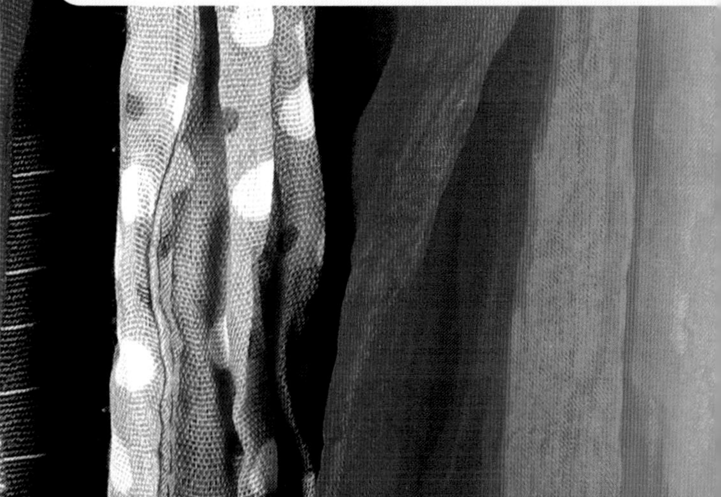

And if you think that this doesn't happen much — wrong. It happens all the time in both advertisements and celebrity magazine photos.

To be fair, some within the fashion industry are trying to move away from this image of perfection, recognizing it as both unrealistic and destructive. Some designers are putting minimum weight criteria on their models, and some advertising campaigns are attempting to use more diverse models of different sizes and shapes in their campaigns.

As of January 2013, Israel requires its models to maintain a healthy BMI of more than 18.5. The new law also says that anyone who digitally alters a photograph to make a model appear thinner than she really is must clearly mark the resulting images so that everyone can see that they have been Photoshopped.[7]

While all good steps in the right direction, the truth is that although most countries have guidelines for the modeling industry, it is generally self-regulated and change is very slow to come. In the meantime, you are still being ruthlessly subjected to a very narrow, very unrealistic definition of beauty.

The Second Side of the Equation: You

So who are the *powers* that set this incredibly ridiculous standard of beauty? Well, that is a hard one to answer. Although many support the ideal, no one actually wants to be held responsible for it. Is it the model, who is just trying to keep her job, the photographer, the designer, the advertiser or you (and me), who actually buy the stuff that is being advertised in this way?

Many advertisers will say that this is what the consumers (us) want to see. We want to see a fantasy of who we could be. Forget that it's not real — we want to dream. If so, that lays a lot of the blame squarely on our shoulders.

Is that true? Perhaps a bit of it is. I mean we do keep buying many of the products designed to re-do us. On the other hand, it can be hard to stand up to all the pressure. It becomes a bit of a vicious circle. What is a girl to do?

You can always work to make the changes you want to see in the world. More than ever, young people have the ability to create powerful change. Your voice is strong. But change takes time and not everybody wants to take on global issues. **So if it is not practical to change the forces around you, concentrate on what you can change — how you let them affect you.**

Here are a few strategies to help you get started.

There will be lots of strategies and ideas discussed in this book. Some you may agree with, some you may not. Not every strategy will work for everyone. That's the beauty. You are smart and unique and know yourself best. So have a read and then decide for yourself. But remember, sometimes it doesn't hurt to just try something new.

For a period of time I got into reading this certain magazine. It is a very popular lifestyle magazine that aims to help its readers (mostly adult women) have happier and more fulfilled lives. Sounds good right?

So, I took to reading this regularly to pick up some useful tips. There were articles on health and beauty, on diet and exercise, on financial planning, on job selection, on parenting, on relationships and lots of other things. I thought I was doing something good for myself, something that would make me a happier, more fulfilled person. But then something unexpected happened.

I began not feeling so good about myself. I began feeling a little less content about my decisions and what I was doing. And I couldn't for the life of me figure out why. And then one day it hit me — BAM — just like that I realized what it was. It was the magazine I had taken to reading!

You might think this was weird since the magazine was intended to make me feel better about myself and it did take me a while to work it out. But when I did, it became clear. You see, the articles in the magazine weren't giving me options or suggestions. They were telling me what I should be doing to "maximize" myself. They were telling me what I should be doing about my job and my finances and my health and my diet and my love life and every other part of my life. I realized that there was no way that I could live up to all of the advice. I just couldn't do it all. I couldn't be "perfectly maximized!" Instead of this magazine self-helping me into feeling better, it was making me feel totally inadequate for not being able to keep up.

You would not believe what a relief it was once I actually realized what it was that was making me feel this way. Once I understood it, I could do something about it. And I did.

You might guess that I stopped reading this magazine. But that's not what I did. I just read it with an understanding of its messages and how they were delivered. I chose only the articles I was interested in. When I read a piece, I considered the advice that was offered and chose to try things that made sense for me, while choosing either not to do things that didn't make sense for me or adapting them to who I am. (I am never going to get up at 6 am and exercise no matter how many experts tell me that it is the best time of day to do this. I am not a morning person.) And I disagreed with some of the advice. Okay, not out loud like a crazy lady talking to the air, but in my head. That's right. It is okay to disagree.

Just because something is on TV or in a magazine (or a book) does not make it automatically right for you. It may be right for someone, but you are not everyone, you are unique.

— Me

1. Understand What You Are Seeing and How It Makes You Feel

Every day, we are exposed to dozens, maybe hundreds, of messages — some visual and some verbal. Often we go through our day without really "seeing" or thinking about these messages and how they make us feel. I hope that my personal story on the opposite page gave you a better understanding of what I mean.

Truly being aware of the messages we encounter and understanding the intent of each one, both individually and as part of a collective campaign, can help to decrease some of the power that they may have over you.

So the next time you walk through the mall and see all those window posters showing perfectly perfect girls looking perfectly happy, don't let the images just wash over you into an unconscious blend of self-criticism because you don't look that happy or that perfect. Truly see what you are seeing and understand how they make you feel. Use your brain, use your knowledge. Recognize that those images are there for one reason only — to get you to buy things. Look closely, you know that those images have been styled and photographed and Photoshopped by the best. This awareness may not make you feel totally great about yourself, but there is a great relief when you finally identify and face the things head on that are affecting you.

2. Be the Best You Can Be

I know that this sounds completely cheesy, and you have heard it before. If you can stop rolling your eyes for just a minute, there is a reason that you have heard this before. It's true! You instantly feel better when you start to take charge of your life in a positive way.

It's like when you have a test that you are really nervous about and the instant you start studying you begin to relax and feel better. It's because you are taking charge of the situation in a meaningful way. Regardless of how you do on the test, you have done your best in studying for it and that makes you feel better and proud of yourself. The same principle applies here.

It's easy to get discouraged when we don't feel good physically. It's easy to just sort of give up and accept the unhappiness. But this can become a vicious cycle. You don't feel good about yourself, so you stop taking care of yourself or start trying to hide yourself, and then you feel worse and so on. Regardless of what's bothering you, eating right and exercising can go a long way to improving the way you feel about yourself overall.

Not only does exercise act as a great stress reliever, but it also releases endorphins (your brain's feel good stuff) and helps improve your sleep (and being well-rested, in and of itself, helps keep you on balance).

The thing about this idea is that it's an easy one to try. The next time you feel discouraged or angry or sad, just try working out for an hour. It doesn't have to be too crazy and you don't need an expensive gym membership, just a bike ride or a jog or a walk around the block will clear your head and your mood.

As soon as you can begin to focus more on your physical self, the better you will feel about yourself, the more time you will spend on yourself and the less focus you will put on comparing yourself to others. And that's a good thing.

3. Let Go

You can choose to accept and celebrate all that you are and move on to the more important areas of your life. You may think that this advice is overly simplistic, that others *just don't understand*. But almost all females understand.

Very few girls or women feel completely secure in their looks even a small part of the time. But you don't have to feel 100% happy with the way you look to feel good about yourself. First of all know that you don't need perfection (remember, it only exists at the end of an airbrush or computer cursor). It's okay to wish you were a little taller, or maybe your nose was slightly different. It's okay to wish you were naturally slimmer or maybe had thicker hair. No one is ever going to be completely satisfied with everything they have. It's not in our natures, so don't feel bad for wishing something was different. If you can make a change that you desire in a healthy way, then great. But, ultimately, to feel good about yourself, you have to accept the things you can't change and move on!

Sometimes it's as simple as just letting it go. That's right, not everything is complicated. Mind over matter works and sometimes you can lift the pressure you feel around you simply by choosing to.

Have you ever just let yourself go? Just done something for fun regardless of how you looked? Ran through the school ground, sang at the top of your lungs, danced uncontrollably just because it was fun? If you haven't lately, you should. That feeling of weightlessness you feel when you are absorbed in something you love can be mastered for your everyday life. You can just choose to let go of the pressures of perfection. You can choose to be comfortable and happy in your own skin just because you want to be. You can choose to concentrate on the things that you enjoy in life, even if you don't look perfect while doing them. You can choose. The mind is an amazing thing.

4. Celebrate the Beauty in Others (It Doesn't Take Away from Your Own)

Another good strategy to follow is to be open to the beauty in others so that you can see the beauty in yourself. Very rarely does a girl have the ability to look upon another's good qualities and appreciate them without making an instant comparison to herself. And this is a big stumbling block to feeling good about ourselves. Although this may be normal, it is a horrible characteristic that most of us have and it actually does us more harm than good.

Yes, it is incredibly hard to be faced with model images daily. Yes, they can absolutely warp what you come to think of as normal and healthy. Yes, faced with such images you can lose track of the fact that beauty is in the eye of the beholder and all types, shapes, sizes and colors of girls are beautiful. Yes, it can suck. But it isn't going to change overnight, and so you have to take some control of your feelings so that you don't end up as one more girl who struggles her whole life with poor self-esteem, 'cause that is an awful life to lead.

And what if changes did happen? Even if the entire industry changed tomorrow, even if thin was no longer in, even if ad campaigns suddenly celebrated all types of beauty, that nasty little habit of self-comparison will still get us if we don't nip it in the bud.

There will always be someone richer, thinner, with thicker hair or longer legs or better grades or faster on the track or, or, or. ... It doesn't matter what the quality. And they don't have to be staring at us from a magazine. They can be walking down the street or sitting next to us in math class. There will always be girls different from you. You are never going to be faced only with your mirror image.

So you need to practice admiring what you like in others without immediately being jealous or making comparisons. For example, the next time you admire something about a girl in school, don't scowl with envy, but compliment her on whatever quality it may be.

"Wow, I love your hair."

"You were really good in the school play."

You will be surprised at how good you feel when you share good feelings with the world. Envy will cripple you; generosity of spirit will make you feel amazing. And as you open your eyes to others, you will begin to notice so many other great things about people that have nothing to do with external perfection.

Along the way, you are going to be able to help a lot of other girls who may also be struggling with their self-image. Imagine how good you would feel if someone just walked up to you and said something nice about you. It might move your thoughts away from concentrating on some of the negative feelings you have about yourself. And as you begin to notice good things in others, a surprising thing will happen.

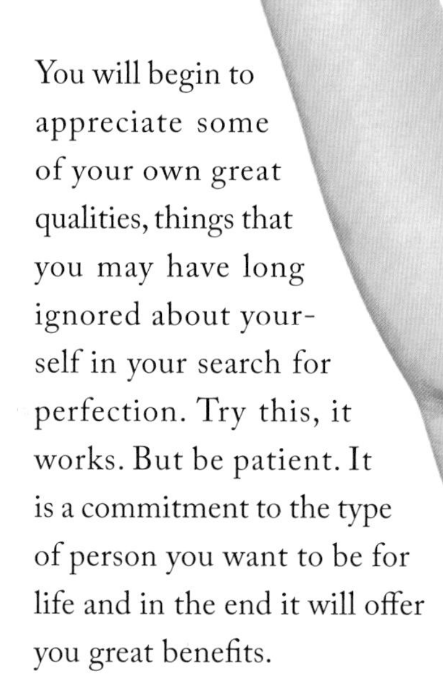

You will begin to appreciate some of your own great qualities, things that you may have long ignored about yourself in your search for perfection. Try this, it works. But be patient. It is a commitment to the type of person you want to be for life and in the end it will offer you great benefits.

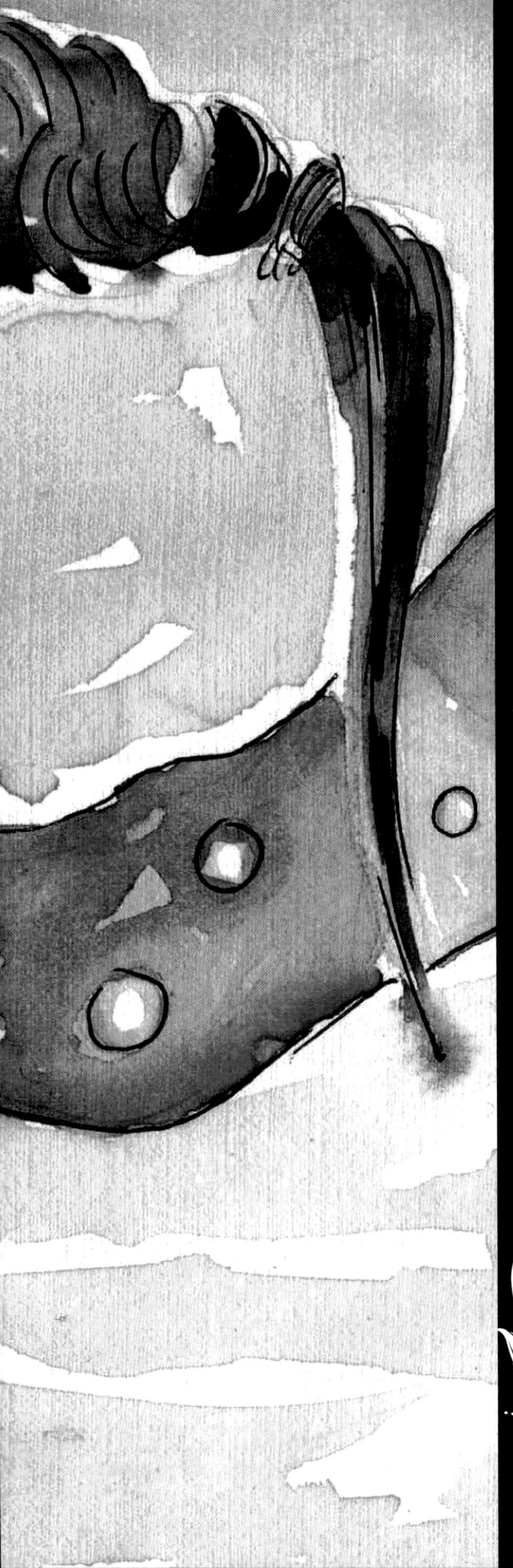

FRIENDS, FRIENEMIES AND FOES

"Why aren't you as thin as your friends?"

"Why aren't you as thin as your friends?"

What does someone say to that? I mean what kind of a question is that? As an adult, I would never say to someone, "Why are your eyes so close together?" I wouldn't ask that for many reasons. First, it implies that there is something wrong with the person's eyes — and that's mean. Second, what kind of an answer am I expecting exactly? Short of a discussion on genetics and DNA, what's the answer I am going for? And why does it matter?

But this is exactly the question that 12-year-old Marie was asked on the school ground one day while hanging out at lunch with her friends. That's right, friends. The remark was made by a boy who Marie was pretty sure wasn't trying to be mean. He just made an observation and asked the question. The result was as you can imagine. While laughing it off and trying to change subjects as quickly as possible, Marie was dying inside. She realized instantly the stupidity of the question, nevertheless it embarrassed her deeply. Not only did he ask the question, but he did so in front of all their friends. The affect was lasting. The embarrassment turned to anger.

She was angry at the boy for asking such a stupid question, but she was angrier that she was not as thin as her friends and this is the anger she turned inside, on herself. When asked why she didn't just tell the boy that was a stupid question, she replied that she couldn't. She was so embarrassed she just wanted to change the subject. Despite being a beautiful, popular, smart, athletic girl, this remark stirred up all her self-doubt and self-loathing. This one question overshadowed, in her mind, all the great things that she was. This one question caused many nights of tears. This one question was asked by a *friend*.

Friendships are important. The friends you have, you wish you had or you used to have are another huge influence in your life and can reinforce how you feel about yourself for good or for bad. The affect that friends can have on you is so powerful, yet sometimes so subtle, that it can be incredibly difficult to navigate through this portion of your life. Everybody wants to be popular, everybody wants to be liked, but at what cost? Only you can determine the answer to that question. As with all the influences in your life, sometimes you need to step outside the emotion of the moment in order to regain some of your balance. While your friends may affect you, they don't have to define you — only you should do that.

Bullying is any unwanted aggressive behavior, where you feel helpless to stop what is going on. It can be as obvious as a punch or as subtle as a whisper. It can leave you feeling scared, angry, alone and helpless. In this Internet generation, where messages and threats can be spread at the speed of light, bullying has taken on epic proportions.

This book is all about the choices that you have in life to define who you want to be and about the power that you have to feel good about yourself. But bullying is not an area to which this applies. As strong as you are, you can't *choose* to change the actions of a bully. A bully's actions speak to who they are, not to who you are.

The choice you have here is to get help if you are a victim of bullying or if you know of someone else who may be suffering. You always have the power to at least reach out for help. Talk to your parents, teacher, coach or anyone and everyone. Don't let a bully frighten you from asking for help. You will be amazed at how many good people there are out there more than willing to help you if you give them the chance.

WHEN FRIENDS HURT

Sometimes it is very difficult to pinpoint the more subtle social influences that may be affecting how you feel about yourself.

Like what if the words that are making you feel ugly or stupid or worthless are coming from a friend? It would be nice if life was like a Disney movie, where your friends were perfect kids, always supportive and inclusive, and the bad kids are so obviously off their rocker that even the neighborhood dog doesn't like them. Unfortunately life is not like that. It's not often a case of good versus bad. Life is much more subtle and that is what can make it so difficult.

I think friendships are great. Personally, I find life is made easier by having friends. But that is not to say that sometimes my friends don't make me mad, hurt or sad. It's just that in the overall cost/benefit analysis, my friends offer me more happiness and support than pain. And like all things in life, if you keep your eyes wide open not only are you less likely to walk into a wall, but you will also be in a better position to see your friendships (and your role in them) through more realistic eyes. Then you will have a greater chance of managing the bad with the good because in all friendships there will be some bumps.

Everyone has heard of the dreaded *frienemy*. This is the wolf dressed in sheep's clothing, the supposed friend who spends her time giving you back-handed compliments or competing with you, usually while professing to be one of your BFFs. These types of friends (or non-friends as the case may be) are toxic. While not as frightening or aggressive as bullies, they can still do significant damage to your self-esteem and must be addressed.

There is some science that says no matter what you do your tween/teen years are predestined to be fraught with drama and pain. It has been argued that the young brain is hardwired to act in a certain way and that brain development and hormonal changes decide to a large extent your behavior. In girls this might include an unstoppable need for gossiping or competition — classic frienemy behavior. However, there has also been scientific research that disputes these claims. Well, I am not a scientist, but neither are you (at least not yet). We don't have to weigh in on this argument. So, I am going old-school here in believing that, while it is true your brain is still developing and your hormones are most likely running amok like a kitten in a catnip factory, you still have the ability to make choices in your life that will ultimately support you and make you feel good about yourself.

There are lots of "tests" floating around about how you can identify if your friend is really a frienemy. But without worrying about the exact label, the easiest way to tell whether a friend is good for you or not is whether you feel better or worse after spending time together. In general, if your interactions with a person continually leave you feeling bad or sad or just not quite right inside, there is a pretty good chance that the relationship has tipped from being a supportive healthy one to one which is better left behind.

But wait a minute ... just because you are having some difficulty with a friend doesn't necessarily mean you have a frienemy in your midst. Perhaps other factors are at play.

1. Like All Things, Friendships Change Over Time

Catharine and Sabrina had been best friends since grade one. You know the drill; they were inseparable on the school ground, sat next to each other on the bus, dressed alike, thought alike, dreamed alike. Sure, they fought once in a while, but they were never truly hurtful to one another and a fight from the day before was quickly forgotten when they reunited the next day in class. As they grew, their interests changed, but they were still always in sync with each other — right up to and including their newfound interest in boys once they hit middle school.

They talked incessantly about which boys they thought were cute, which couples were going to go to the dance together, who was with who and who broke up with who, who they liked and who might like them (all the stuff that is way more important in middle school than the actual *school* part). But all this changed when Sabrina got her first boyfriend — Brian.

All of a sudden, a lot of Sabrina's time was taken up with Brian — hanging out at school, walking home together, talking at night. Well you can see where this is going; Catharine felt left out, angry and unimportant to Sabrina. But more than that, Catharine felt ugly and unwanted because she didn't have a boyfriend of her own. And she targeted all of these feelings right at Sabrina. It was Sabrina's fault.

You might be thinking what a crappy friend Sabrina was, throwing over her best friend since grade one all for the sake of a boy. That's exactly what Catharine thought. That is how Catharine justified her own feelings of self-loathing. "It was Sabrina's fault she felt this way about herself!" But is it true? Was everything Catharine feeling Sabrina's fault?

I mean, it's hard not to take the side of orphaned puppies.

After two people spend so much time together, it's hard to accept when one of them begins to need some of that time back to spend on other interests. This would be true regardless of what the time is needed for. Sabrina's new interest was a boyfriend, but what if it had been because she decided to train for the Olympics or to spend her time helping orphaned puppies find new homes. I mean Catharine sounds justified when she is angry at Sabrina over a boy, but would people sympathize as much with Catharine if Sabrina was training for an internationally loved event or helping orphaned puppies? I mean, it's hard not to take the side of orphaned puppies.

The point is that it's not always why the relationship is changing that is important; it's how it changed that needs to be considered. If Sabrina completely cut Catharine out when she started seeing Brian and then, once her relationship with Brian ended, Sabrina expected Catharine to devote all her time back to the friendship only to completely ignore Catharine once again the next time she got a boyfriend, then yes, this type of behavior could be influencing how Catharine felt about herself and her own worth and she may have to make a choice to end the friendship. But that's not exactly what happened in this case.

Yes, Sabrina did not have *as much time* for Catharine (there are only so many hours in the day), but while Catharine felt thrown aside, Sabrina honestly tried to balance her time as much as possible. She still saved the seat beside her for Catharine in the lunch room, called her at night (for a little less time, but she still checked in). Sabrina even invited Catharine several times to hang with her and Brian, something Catharine chose not to do. But Catharine didn't see any of this. She only saw that Sabrina had changed their relationship. Things were different, Catharine didn't feel good about herself and it was all Sabrina's fault.

The truth is things change ... and if they didn't life would get very boring. Knowing this doesn't necessarily make change any easier, but it is a fact of life nonetheless. As you and your friends grow, your interests and circumstances will likely diverge

at points. A friend develops an interest in drama and begins spending more time working on the school play, or gets a boyfriend, or moves to a different school, or, or, or. There are lots of great things going on in life, things that will require time to pursue. Because a friend suddenly needs or wants to spend some time following a new interest doesn't, in and of itself, mean that person is not a good friend anymore or reflect on their feelings toward you.

If you are the Catharine of this story, the one who is feeling left behind and hurt, before you let your anger over-run you, consider your role in the relationship. Try to objectively see what is going on. Have you really been completely dismissed or is your friend just asking for a little time and space to develop new interests? Are you so busy feeling sorry for yourself that you are not being supportive of your friend's new adventure? Friendship is a two way street. Is there a way you can meet in the middle so that both your needs are being fulfilled? And honestly, is it so bad to be left with a little more time to yourself? While it is great to be social, if you are not comfortable in your own company then you are going to continually run into problems.

In this case Catharine also blamed Sabrina for her own self-esteem issues. By Sabrina having a boyfriend, it punctuated Catharine's feelings about herself, but was this really a fair thing to lay at Sabrina's door? Sabrina had never said an unkind word to Catharine about her looks or her abilities.

As with all things in life, it is hard to figure out ways to handle a situation if you don't first look honestly at what is going on, which leads to the next point worth considering.

2. The Truth Can Hurt

A good friend can tell you what is the matter with you in a minute.
He may not seem such a good friend after telling.

—Arthur Brisbane

When a supposed friend tells you something out of jealousy or meanness, then there is a good chance that person may be more frienemy than friend. Other times a friend can say something that might hurt, when really they only had the intention of helping you. The trick comes in distinguishing between the two. Although you probably have pretty good radar to help you tell the difference, sometimes, during these years when insecurities (and hormones) are heightened, the radar gets switched off and you may react to every unflattering comment or constructive criticism like someone just stuck a knife in your back.

Although it may seem at times, especially if your self-esteem is a little low, that every critical word is designed solely to hurt you, it is not always the case. Just saying, before you ditch a friend because their words hurt, just make sure you know if the words are coming from their hate or their heart.

3. Sometimes People Are just Stupid

This is a universal fact of life. Sometimes people aren't trying to be mean, they just don't think about how their words or actions will affect another. Sometimes a friend may just have a brain-fart and say something unintentionally mean or sometimes they might just be socially oblivious. Either way, the result can still be hard to take.

When I was 13, there were a bunch of us at a friend's house getting ready for a school dance. One of the girls came out of the bathroom and asked how she looked. In hindsight, I should have just said, "Great." But I didn't. She was wearing her hair up, and I said that I liked it better when she wore her hair down. To this day I remember this because I couldn't believe how fast she got mad.

I don't even remember what she said, but it wasn't nice — a lot of things about what a mean person I was for saying that, etc. And I mean full

something so little. And then I got mad! I hadn't even said anything mean. I had just made an observation. I honestly didn't realize the weight my words would carry. I honestly thought I was paying her a compliment about how nice her hair looked naturally.

Years later that girl finally told me why she had reacted that way. She said she had always felt so insecure about her looks in school that sometimes even the smallest comment would feel like everyone was judging her. Looking at her back then, I wouldn't have guessed that in a million years.

Again I ask, what do you say when someone asks you why you are not as thin as your friends? The easiest answer is to retort with something stunningly clever like, "Why are you stupider than all your friends?" But that isn't going to help your self-esteem. Plus, as Marie said in the opening story, sometimes you are so embarrassed you just want to escape the situation as quickly as possible (which won't happen if you launch into a war of words).

Now, don't get me wrong, stupidity is not a defense for hurting someone, but occasionally it happens and you are going to have to decide how to handle it. Truth is, there is no magic answer — or at least I don't know of one.

If it is a "one off" then you might decide to just let it go. You have to pick your battles in life, and sometimes battling against every wrong, even if justified, is exhausting. There is nothing wrong with letting things go once in a while if that is your decision.

But if you really can't let it go, then don't let it fester. You can speak to the person in a private moment. It can be enough just to let someone know how they are making you feel. They might not realize that what they said was hurtful. A lot of stupid things have been said by someone who thinks they are incredibly insightful or funny. But don't expect even your best friend to be a mind reader. If you don't tell them what is on your mind, how can they know to change their behavior or even apologize? I'm not suggesting you face the school bully, but if you can't talk openly and honestly to your friends, exactly what kind of a friendship do you have? This will serve you well for the rest of your life — be respectful, but be honest and *communicate*.

But beware of the old "it's not me, it's you" defense. Don't fall for this. If someone says something stupid or mean, don't let them convince you that there is something wrong with you for calling them out. "What? Can't take a joke?" is a favorite reply from many people when they get called out on a wrongdoing. Stand up for yourself, just like you would stand up for a friend. If you really feel that what was said (or done) was wrong, then you need to stand firm. You do not want to be that person who keeps everyone happy by allowing them to use you as the butt of their jokes. I can tell you for sure, that type of friendship is not worth it and is going to leave you feeling horrible about yourself.

Only you can decide whether someone has crossed the line from just being stupid to being intentionally hurtful. Only you can decide how many times you are going to accept the stupidity excuse from a friend. Remember that friendships, for the most part, are supposed to make you feel good. If you are consistently feeling bad after spending time with someone, then that is telling you something right there. And nothing will change unless you change it.

4. When Bad Days Happen to Good People

Sometimes, good people do bad things.

It could be as small as your friend just broke up with her boyfriend and is so angry that she yells at you in the middle of the school hall for nothing.

Or it could be something bigger as when your friend is so afraid of getting suspended from school for a repeat offence that in a moment of panic tells the principal you were to blame when you had nothing to do with the event.

What are you going to do? I don't know, that is up to you. The offense might be so bad that you feel you could never forgive or forget. Sometimes it happens that good friendships just can't make it past a mistake. It's sad but true.

But before you write off a friend, consider the long-term relationship. It's wickedly hard to put yourself in someone else's shoes, to understand why they would do something so hurtful. And sometimes you may have to accept that you won't truly ever understand. If that friend is truly sorry, then it is also okay to forgive. Just keep yourself open. Your friend might actually be trying to ask for help through their weird behavior. Be open enough that you don't miss the signs. They might really need you right now.

5. But Sometimes Something Bad Is just the Beginning and You Need to Cut and Run

When writing the previous section I was very concerned that you might misinterpret what I was saying to mean that as long as someone apologized and was sorry for what they did, then you should accept their apology. So I need to be very, very clear

This is something my absolute best friend did. A bunch of us were planning a movie night. We had planned it a whole week before. I was so excited. I even got my parents to cancel family plans that night. When the day came, I found out that we weren't going anymore because my (best) friend had changed the night to the night before with everyone and didn't tell me. I didn't even find out about it until the next day when I talked to the other kids that went. They all just assumed I had known about the change and couldn't make it.

I spent that whole night crying. I felt like such a loser, like no one even cared about me or if I was there or not. I have never felt more worthless in my life.

She eventually apologized, but to this day I have no idea why she did that. It was just mean, pure and simple. But it was a big eye opener. I eventually (with some help) realized that the whole thing spoke to what kind of a person she was at the time; it had nothing to do with me.

That happened a year ago, and we've both changed since then. We are still friends. But I'm not sure that I completely trust her anymore and I've realized that I need to work on other friendships so that I don't rely on just one best friend for everything.

— T

on this point. I know that I keep saying that the *choice is yours*, but, in this one area, I am actually saying what I absolutely think you should do.

If a person physically hurts you or is abusive in any way, then the rules change and there is no longer a gray area to consider.

This is especially true when it comes to dating violence. I don't know your actual age, so talking about boyfriends can mean anything. It might just mean that you walk down the school hall together or it might mean that you spend time together at the movies or other places alone.

"Whoa," you might be saying, "I'm not into dating yet." But the truth is, as soon as you are old enough to see boys as anything more than just annoying creatures who snort chocolate milk through their noses, you are old enough to understand this issue.

While dating violence can go either way (in other words, boys can be assaulted by girls), the truth is that girls are much more likely to be the ones assaulted in a violent relationship. And since this book is for you, this is what we are going to talk about.

While the statistics differ depending on the survey, the truth is undeniable. This is a serious issue. Dating abuse can be physical, sexual or emotional. No amount of abuse during a relationship is tolerable.

Other than the obvious signs (he hits you), there are other signs that a relationship is only going to go from bad to worse.

Here are some warning signs.

- If he is overly jealous. Despite fairy-tale notions to the contrary, jealousy is not a romantic quality and does not show how much he loves you; it demonstrates his own insecurities.

- If he doesn't trust you and is always asking you to provide details of where you were and who you were with.
- If he demands control of your behavior — the way you act or dress or the activities you get involved with or your opinions.
- If he tries to isolate you from your friends or family.
- If you are always nervous that you might say or do the wrong thing when you are with him and make him mad.
- If you have gone from being relatively happy and carefree to being scared and feeling trapped.

You are an amazing girl. And you are smart. But sometimes you might get into a situation that is difficult to handle alone, especially when so many emotions are involved. If you truly feel that you love someone, it can be very difficult to end a relationship, especially if that person is telling you how much they love you and how sorry they are; how much they have changed or will change; or, worse yet, that they will hurt you or themselves if you leave.

In this situation you really need to follow your head and not your heart. And **beware these myths that you could fall victim to if you don't keep your eyes wide open.**

- *This Is Normal.* Maybe because you are new to this or, worse, maybe because you have been exposed to this in other areas of your life, you might think that this is what a normal relationship is like, that this is just the way boys are. It is not. A normal, healthy, good relationship is one in which you feel supported and respected. You have a lot of chances for great relationships; don't set a bad one as the benchmark.

- *Love Conquers All.* It is a romantic notion that if you just love the person more, they will change. Unfortunately in real life it doesn't work that way. Abusers need serious, qualified help. All your love in the world won't change the situation.

- *I Can't Just Walk Away; It Would Be Mean.* Yes, you can just walk away and, no, it would not be mean. Even if that person threatens to harm himself, it is not your responsibility to stay in the relationship and try to fix things. You can have compassion, you can steer him (with help) to the counseling he needs, but you can't fix it on your own. An abusive person needs help that you just cannot provide. In this case, you need to take care of yourself first and know that it is okay to do so.

- *He Really Does Love Me.* The reality is that an abuser is not capable of real love, a love in which they want only the best for the other person. I won't pretend to understand all of the complicated factors that can cause one person to abuse another, but I do understand that no matter how many gut-wrenching apologies and over-the-top gifts and proclamations of love, an abuser is not capable of a healthy, loving relationship without serious professional help.

- *Things Will Improve Over Time; We just Hit a Couple of Bumps.* Abuse isn't a bump and such behavior won't spontaneously disappear. Once you show that you will accept this type of behavior then things will only get worse. The sooner you get out of this type of relationship the better.

- *It's the Best I Deserve.* It is heartbreaking to think that a young girl could have such low self-esteem that she would think that she deserves no better than abusive treatment. Unfortunately it happens all too frequently. Girls who are so insecure and so afraid of never having a boyfriend can truly believe that this is as good as it gets. But this is not true. You deserve so much; you are worth so much more than this. This is one of the reasons it is so important to work on your self-esteem at this point in your life. You need to respect yourself so that you can demand that respect from others. Even if you sit home on a few Saturday nights now, it will pay off big in the future.

So please, please, please, please, if you are in an abusive dating relationship or think that a friend of yours might be, then get help from a trusted adult. Violence never disappears on its own.

Forty percent of girls aged 14 to 17 report knowing someone their age who has been hit or beaten by a boyfriend. (Children Now/Kaiser Permanente poll, December 1995)

In a recent survey, 9.4% of high school students report being hit, slapped, or physically hurt on purpose by their boyfriend or girlfriend in the 12 months prior to the survey. (Centers for Disease Control and Prevention, *2011 Youth Risk Behavior Survey)*.

Among 11-14 year olds who have been in a relationship:

- A strong majority (62%) say they know friends who have been verbally abused (called stupid, worthless, ugly, etc.) by a boyfriend/girlfriend.
- More than a third (36%) know friends and peers their age who have been pressured by a boyfriend/girlfriend to do things they didn't want to do.
- One in four tweens say dating violence is a serious problem for people their age.
- **Still, only half of all tweens (51%) claim to know the warning signs of a bad/hurtful tween-dating relationship.**

(Liz Claiborne Inc., *Tween Relationships Study* (2008))

"SO WHAT POWER DO I HAVE EXACTLY?"

You have a lot of power if you choose to use it because in most situations in your life, if you really think about it, you do have a choice.

- You can choose to stand up for yourself.
- You can choose to focus on all the great things about yourself.
- You can choose to walk away from relationships that don't respect who you are.

The problem is that most of us don't exercise this power, because it can be a very hard thing to do.

When it comes to your social life, you have the power to spend time with the people who will most often support, respect and make you feel good about yourself. I mean not always, people aren't angels or anything, but at least for the most part you can choose to center your relationships on those who honestly see what an amazing person you are, just the way you are.

Friends aren't perfect, but then again, neither are you. But if you keep your eyes open, you will be in a better position to know which relationships generally support you and which are leaving you (more than not) feeling not very good about yourself. You can choose to look at your relationships honestly and make changes when necessary, even if it involves some short-term sacrifices.

This is not an easy thing to do, especially at your age when all your friendships tend to be tied together and your social circle takes on the power to define who you are, both to yourself and to others. But it doesn't have to be this way. You can choose to define yourself and not let others do it for you.

Friends aren't perfect, but then again, neither are you.

11 TIPS TO HELP YOU THROUGH

1. You Are Not Alone

When we are the most down, it is so easy to think that no one else in the world is experiencing or has ever experienced our depths of anger or sadness or embarrassment or despair. In reality, nothing could be further from the truth. You might not always see it in others because they hide it as well as you do, but know that you are not the only one struggling with trying to fit in.

It doesn't matter how happy or confident everyone else may look to you, almost all young people, at different times, have felt the same self-doubt. They may handle it differently than you. Some may become aggressive, some competitive, some super-pleasing, some withdrawn, but remember, when you are feeling awkward and uncomfortable in your own skin that you are not the only one. When you are struggling with decisions, others are also struggling. When you have been so embarrassed by an incident that you never again want to leave your room, know that almost everyone has felt this way (and more than once). When you feel alone and friendless, there are other girls who feel just the same way.

If nothing else, always remember that there is nothing "wrong" with you.

2. It's Hard, but Sometimes You just Have to Walk Away

What happens when you are having problems with one person that is tied into a whole group of friends? This can be a really difficult problem, especially at school, where you tend to form groups of friends. A group can be a great thing because it's fun to hang out with a lot of people and there is always someone around to be with. But it depends what kind of group it is.

If it is an autocratic group, one in which there is a clear leader calling all the shots and you aren't feeling good about that friendship, then, although it is difficult, you may have to give up the whole gang in order to be true to yourself. In a situation like this, others are often following the leader because they, too, are feeling insecure and afraid to be out of the group. Maybe just seeing you stand up for yourself will be enough to encourage others in the group to also take a stand. This won't always happen, so you have to be prepared to go it alone for a while until you find better, stronger friendships. One thing for sure is you are never going to have the opportunity for great friendships if you are afraid to stand on your own and look for them.

If everyone in your group gets along well, and you have many great friendships within the gang, but are just having problems with one member, then it can be trickier to figure out how to navigate

I hung around with a really good group of friends in school. There were seven of us and I liked them and didn't really have too many problems with any of them, except for one. For some reason, this girl always made comments about me, not behind my back or anything, right to my face, but always in front of other people. She always said them as if joking. I don't know why I was her target.

One remark that I remember was her pointing out the size of my hands. She said that they were so big they were like shovels. I know that this is not a huge thing, but still, I was already self-conscious about my hands, so even years later, this comment stuck.

But, I really liked all the other girls in the group and we had tons of fun, so I just decided that this one relationship wasn't going to spoil the whole thing. So I learned to ignore her comments to the point where eventually I barely heard them and they didn't bother me anymore. And the funny thing is that soon enough, she was only embarrassing herself because everyone else started to realize how petty and mean she could be.

— C

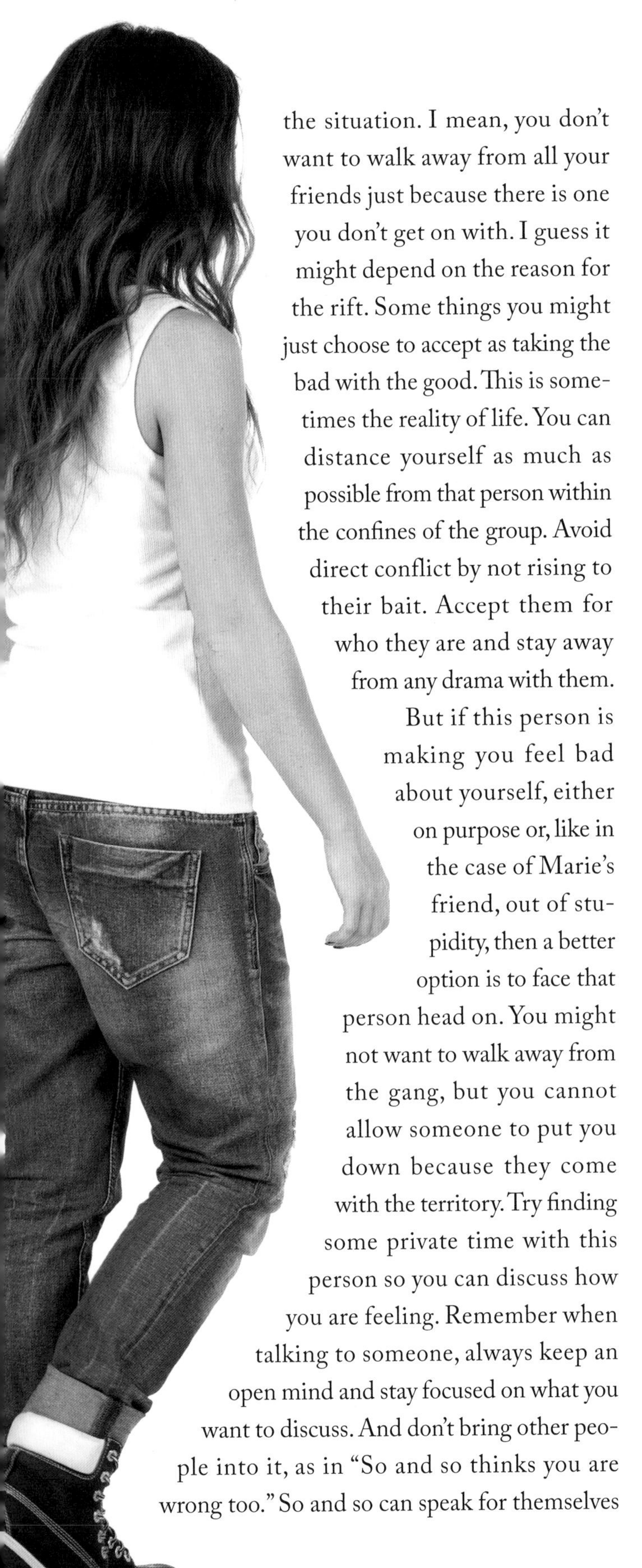

the situation. I mean, you don't want to walk away from all your friends just because there is one you don't get on with. I guess it might depend on the reason for the rift. Some things you might just choose to accept as taking the bad with the good. This is sometimes the reality of life. You can distance yourself as much as possible from that person within the confines of the group. Avoid direct conflict by not rising to their bait. Accept them for who they are and stay away from any drama with them.

But if this person is making you feel bad about yourself, either on purpose or, like in the case of Marie's friend, out of stupidity, then a better option is to face that person head on. You might not want to walk away from the gang, but you cannot allow someone to put you down because they come with the territory. Try finding some private time with this person so you can discuss how you are feeling. Remember when talking to someone, always keep an open mind and stay focused on what you want to discuss. And don't bring other people into it, as in "So and so thinks you are wrong too." So and so can speak for themselves if they feel the need. Plus, not only do you lose credibility if so and so doesn't back up your claim, but the other person is going to feel attacked and a lot less likely to be open to working on the problem. Stand up for yourself, but maintain your class. Ultimately you will always feel better about yourself, whether the situation resolves or not, if you are proud of the way you acted.

3. Don't be Afraid of Spending Time with Yourself

If you make friends with yourself,
you will never be alone.

— Maxwell Maltz

I like this quote. If you brush it off for being corny, re-read it and think about the power it is offering you. Now don't get me wrong, I think a life is much richer when you are surrounded by good people, but notice that there is an adjective. It's not enough just to be surrounded by people. Better to be on your own than to spend time with people who don't support and respect you or, worse yet, actually make you feel bad about yourself.

I know at this age everything is defined by how many friends you have or how popular you are, and while friends are great, **be careful of the trap of needing to always be included in order to feel good about yourself.** Girls who always need to have a boyfriend or always need to be part of the group will give up a lot of themselves in order to fulfill this need. Think about it. If you are not willing to walk away from a friend or group that makes you feel bad, then what power do you have to control your own life? If you can't change them and you won't leave, how is anything going to get better for you?

Sure, you might have to spend a few evenings on your own for a bit, but is this really so bad? You might immediately break out in a cold sweat, thinking that your whole life is ruined and you are destined to spend the rest of your days alone with a multitude of cats — but wait — stop — breathe.

Instead of immediately going to the negative over some alone time, try going to the positive. Think of this extra time as a gift to do with what you would like. Like a little vacation, this free time won't last forever, so what would you like to do with it? Maybe just relax, maybe get caught up on some hobbies, maybe (gasp!) hang out with your family or maybe connect with some long-lost friends who you haven't had much time for lately. I know that all of these ideas don't center on you being alone, but the idea isn't that you have to be alone, just that you can't be afraid to spend time with only yourself once in a while.

4. Know that Labels Aren't People

Here is something that you might not yet realize. Do you know what *cool* is? Independence is cool. Confidence is cool. I'm going to say something here that I know is going to get me into a lot of trouble and may make you mad. But give me a minute and listen to what I'm saying. You don't have to agree with it, but at least listen.

Many kids aren't cool. Many kids spend the majority of their time worrying about what group they hang with. They want the *label* of the group not the actual people who come with the group. They want to be with the popular group, the pretty group, the smart group, even the *cool* group (however that is defined on any given day). But as soon as you start chasing a label, you have given up a lot of the control of your life to others. If you need to be defined by your social circle, if all that you are is wrapped up in the label of your group, then where is your independence, where is your confidence to stand alone, how are you going to make good decisions for yourself if you are afraid of jeopardizing your place in *the group*?

This isn't to say that you shouldn't make friends with kids who are labeled as popular or smart or cool. If these are good people who you want to spend time with, then great. But don't limit yourself to defining others by their label and choosing your friendships based on these labels. See people for the individuals they really are, just

Not all labels are good, but sometimes people have no control over the labels they get. They are given to them by others without any thought or care and then spread like wildfire through ignorance and meanness. Remember, behind every label there is a person with real feelings just like yours.

Really cool people can see the amazing qualities in all shapes, sizes and types of others.

as you want people to see you for who you really are. Don't define yourself or others by some superficial quality or label. Really cool people can see the amazing qualities in all shapes, sizes and types of others.

5. Take a Break from the Drama Once in a While

Even in the best friendships, there will always be some drama. Beware, drama is exhausting and can leave you feeling yucky (a technical term) without you even realizing why. I know that a little drama and gossip can be fun; some will even argue that we as humans are hardwired to need some drama in our lives, but there is a limit. Whether it's drama you've created yourself, or that of others that you have been drawn into, you need to know when enough is enough and just walk away. Sure you want to be there to comfort a friend, but if that friend is always overly upset about the same thing, or not willing to accept real help, or actually enjoying all of the attention, then maybe you have a drama queen on your hands. Not to say that you have to walk away from that friendship, but you at least have to recognize it for what it is and not get emotionally spent yourself trying to fix everything. Sometimes, you just have to let go and let other people fix their own issues.

And gossip, while it can seem fun in the immediate, is also an incredibly toxic thing to get caught up in. Everyone is taught not to spread gossip, but even listening to a lot of gossip can make you feel kind of dirty and mean inside, because basically gossip is mean spirited. Sometimes you might need to talk to someone about a problem you are having with another person. And once in a while, you just need to vent to a friend about something that happened with a different friend. Although you are talking about a third person in their absence in these scenarios, you are trying to find a solution to a problem.

Gossip, however, is a whole different kettle of fish. When you gossip about someone, you aren't looking for a solution to a problem; you are looking to feel better about yourself at someone else's expense. You are either judging someone, laughing at someone, or spreading rumors out of spite behind someone else's back. It's pointless and it usually has nothing directly to do with you. If you are actually having problems with a person, then you need to talk to that person directly or walk away from them all together. Always talking about them behind their back won't serve to correct any situation.

But you don't have to believe me, this is an easy one to test for yourself. Just take a break from it once in a while and see if you don't feel better about yourself. You don't have to be superior to your friends by announcing that you are too good to gossip, just quietly exit the conversation or steer the conversation onto a more worthwhile topic (like the cool new movie you just saw). This isn't about you becoming a saint, it's just about concentrating on the positive energy in life because once that energy starts to flow throughout you, you will be amazed at how much better you feel about yourself.

6. Remember, Stuff Happens

Accidently burping in front of the boy you like; not realizing that you have leaked during your period and walking around with a red stain on the back of your butt all day; blurting out something incredibly stupid in front on the whole class by mistake; having a wardrobe malfunction in gym class and exposing parts of you that you did not want exposed, … there are a million things that can and will happen to you during your lifetime that will just make you want to instantaneously combust. Embarrassing moments are going to happen to you in life — a lot! And wouldn't it be great if you could handle all of those embarrassing moments like they do on the TV shows? Every week on those comedy shows the lead character seems to do something incredibly embarrassing in front of the whole school and be able to just laugh it off. They are like Teflon — nothing sticks.

While that would be an amazing way to be, it's hard to laugh off everything in real life. More likely you are going to want to dig a hole and throw yourself in until everyone you know has grown and moved away. But that is not realistic either. So you are going to have to find a balance somewhere between these two.

Sometimes you just have to put the moment into perspective. Let's say you fart in front of the class in the middle of your science presentation. You know that is going to get around the whole school pretty quickly. Okay, true that's pretty embarrassing. The first thing is to put this into perspective. You didn't kill anyone, you didn't even hurt anyone. Your family is not going to desert you, leaving you homeless and alone. Your good friends will tease and laugh at you (come on, it was pretty funny), but they will still be your friends. Some of the kids might tease you mercilessly and never let you forget, but you knew those people were jerks anyway. The truth is you didn't do anything bad and you have nothing to be ashamed of — embarrassing moments happen to *everyone*. Number one rule to always remember: *You are not alone*. If anyone ever tries to let on that everything they say and do is always perfect, I can tell you for a fact that they are lying.

So something incredibly embarrassing has happened and you don't feel like you will ever be able to show your face again, or that the world will never be the same again. Well, you do have to show your face eventually and the world will return to normal — trust me. But in the meantime, you might have to ride out a few days of jokes at your expense. The trick is not to take it too seriously. Put it into proportion — there are far more serious issues in the world than reciting your school monologue with spinach in your teeth. It might not immediately make you feel better, but *perspective* is a great tool to help get you back on track. Face the embarrassment, hold your head high, laugh at yourself, let go

One of the first few times I got my period, I had a sleepover to go to. I was nervous because I was still inexperienced with handling everything with my period, but I really didn't want to miss the sleepover. So I went and everything was going fine, until I had to go to the washroom and change my pad.

I didn't really realize back then that I wasn't supposed to flush a pad down the toilet. I didn't want to put it in the garbage in case anyone found it. (I don't know why I felt that none of my friends could know that I had my period. It's not like I was the only one this was going to happen to.) So I attempted to flush this huge night-time pad down the toilet and, to my utter horror, not only did it not flush, but the entire system backed up and overflowed all over the place.

This thing I was trying to keep so secret ended with everyone in the bathroom trying to stop the house from flooding!

— B

It doesn't get more embarrassing than this. Picture this. It was my uncle's funeral. There was complete silence in the church and then, without warning, I let out this long squeal of a fart that I just could not stop. There was no hiding it!

— V

of the moment and move on because this is just one moment in a very long life that is going to be full of lots of embarrassing moments — and great moments too.

(And by the way, the next time you see another suffering through an embarrassing moment, voluntarily help lighten their load by making a supportive joke or talking about a similar thing that happened to you or anything else you would have liked someone to do for you when you were in that situation.)

7. Expand Your World

Whether you are dealing with issues of a friendship that you have or don't have, problems can be a little less devastating and kept in better perspective if you have other things going on in your life as well. If all of your happiness is defined by one narrow element in your life, as soon as you hit a hiccup it can feel as though everything in your world is falling apart. Small dramas can become big if they are all you have to focus on. Get involved in lots of things with lots of different people, so that you always have some balance to your life. Here are a few ideas.

- *Keep Your Circle of Friends Wide.* Sure you may have a best friend, but in general terms, the more the better. Different friends will offer you different opportunities to share different interests. And if one friend suddenly moves or needs to spend some of their time on other things, you won't feel suddenly so all alone.
- *Get Involved with Extra-Curricular Activities that You Enjoy.* Not all of your friends are going to enjoy everything that you do, but don't let that stop you from getting involved with different activities on your own. If you like acting, get involved with the school drama department — or sports, or an art class or anything else you want to try. You might meet some new people that become great friends, or not. You might just enjoy doing the activity for yourself.
- *Get Involved with the Community.* There are lots of great volunteer activities in communities and nothing makes you get over your problems quicker than when you are out in the world helping others.
- *Spend Some Time with Those who Love You Unconditionally.* It might not be as cool to hang with your family or grandparents or siblings, but a great way to rebalance yourself and remember that you have a whole world apart from your social circle is to spend some time with those people who are always there for you and love you just the way you are.

I was in grade six and lived in a neighborhood full of kids. A whole gang of us was out playing one evening, including a boy that I really liked. I was having lots of fun — a little too much fun. Someone made a joke, and I start laughing so hard that I peed myself. To this day I remember the peeing, but can't for the life of me remember the reaction of any of the kids.

— J

8. It's Okay to Have a Bad Day Once in a While

You are going to have some great days when you feel completely confident in yourself and everything just clicks with your friends and you are on top of the world, but you are also going to have some really bad days when you feel awful about yourself and nothing is working out right and you feel like you don't have a friend in the world. It just happens. It happens to everyone. It's okay.

You just have to ride through some bad days. And there is nothing wrong with recognizing that you are having a bad day and indulging yourself a little to get through it. It's okay to feel sorry for yourself once in a while, to have a good cry, to want to cuddle up alone in the safety of your bedroom and ignore the world. There is nothing wrong with a little self-indulgence on occasion. Everyone needs to do this sometimes. Let yourself and your worries go for an evening. Don't try to solve everything. You don't have to be completely strong all of the time. Sometimes you are just going to be overwhelmed and tired and that's okay.

Eventually you will have to shake it off and get up and on with your life. More often than not, the next day will naturally be better, but not always. Sometimes, whatever issue has sent you into the dumps won't disappear overnight. That doesn't mean that you should stay holed up in your room forever, feeling bad. While a good cry can be very therapeutic, continually feeling sorry for yourself is not the way to lead your life.

9. Don't Forget to Laugh at Yourself Now and Then

Personally, nothing can take me from a slow simmer to a fast boil quicker than when someone tells me to "lighten up." It's kind of like poking a hungry bear. The truth is though that life is short and sometimes all of us could benefit from laughing a little more at ourselves and not taking everything so seriously.

There are certain days when I just don't have this ability. I'm in a bad mood, look out! I may explode in a firestorm or burst into tears at one wrong glance. Fair enough, everyone gets moody sometimes. But overall, you can choose to live your life with a little less drama and a little more laughter. You don't need to let people walk all over you, and certainly don't let others make fun of you, but you also don't have to look for the hidden meaning behind every innocent comment.

Sometimes a joke is just a joke and it's okay to laugh.

10. You Know Yourself and that's What Counts Most

Sometimes things might be said about you that aren't true. Maybe you made a mistake and did something stupid, or maybe out of spite someone has started a nasty rumor about you or maybe people just misunderstood something that happened. Try as you might, you just can't change the perception people have of you right now.

It will take an unbelievable act of strength sometimes, but you can't stop believing in yourself despite what others may think. Even if you have made a mistake and somehow contributed to what people are thinking, don't lose sight of who you really are.

If you have done something where you think you were wrong, then own up to it and apologize. If there is a misperception about something you have done, then you can try to clear it up. If you have made a mistake, then admit it. But ultimately, if people want to continue to think the worst despite your efforts, there may be little that you can do, except to continue to be true to yourself.

And if you are true to yourself, others will eventually see that. And for those who don't, well, that is their problem not yours. The most important thing is that you can lay your head down on your pillow at night knowing that you are a good person. Be strong and believe in yourself. You are amazing.

11. Be Who You Expect Others to Be

It's a message that is simple, direct and to the point. Be the type of person to others that you want them to be to you. You can't expect others to be kind and forgiving and supportive of you if you are not willing to be that way yourself. So, every once in a while, stop and take a good look at yourself. Sometimes we get so caught up in finding faults in others, or being hurt by the actions of others, that we take no time to consider how we are behaving. The easiest thing in the world is to get hurt or angry at someone and then take that hurt and anger out on someone else — spreading the dirt around. Or wanting our friends to acknowledge us, show us that they value us, but never doing that for them.

I know that this has been mentioned before, but if you want people to celebrate who you are, then start by celebrating them. Lead the trend! And even if you don't get back tit for tat, the payback will still be tenfold, because, girl, will you feel good about yourself when you put your head down on that pillow at night.

When I was 13, there was a boy that I really liked. He said that he really liked me too, and asked me to send a photo of myself to him. I don't know why I did it, I was just so happy that this guy liked me, so I sent him a topless picture of myself.

It was stupid and I regret it more than I can say. He showed the picture to all his friends, and pretty soon it got all around the school that I had done all these things with him and lots of other boys too, even though none of that was true. They said I was a slut and the girls started treating me badly. I wish I could take it back, but I can't. I'm not that type of girl, I just made a mistake.

— J

BOYS, BOYS, BOYS

I have a beautiful girl, and every time a boy says something mean to her, I feel her anger and frustration. I also have a beautiful boy, and every time a girl breaks his heart I feel his pain and loneliness. Loving both, I obviously do not believe that boys are inherently any meaner than girls. Boys can be just as wonderful and supportive and giving as any girl, but it doesn't mean that's necessarily the side you are going to see right now. The truth is that boys are going through much the same thing as you are at this age — insecurity, low self-esteem and feelings of uncertainty. They are exposed to the same social pressures and expectations that you are exposed to. It is tough to be a girl faced with flawless model images of perfection, but it is also tough to be a boy faced with rugged, action hero, never-let-them-see-you-hurt images of manliness and strength.

Just like you don't wake up looking like you have just stepped off the pages of *Teen Vogue*, so too in real life, boys cannot ward off an evil robot invasion from outer space utilizing their NASA-like knowledge of technology, NASCAR-like driving skills and ninja-like ability to deflect the most advanced weaponry, all the while looking incredibly cool, with buff biceps and perfectly gelled hair. In reality, just like you, boys are facing raging hormones, bodies that don't look like the movie hero's they see on screen, faces full of pimples and countless other insecurities and fears about the world around them.

When I speak to young girls, they seem genuinely shocked about this fact. It often doesn't dawn on them that their words could have the same effect on a boy's self-esteem as a boy's words have on theirs. Girls, who will cry foul about a boy's insensitivity, have no problem in telling him he has "chicken arms" as a joke. Somehow, it is understood that these insults just aren't as serious and that boys, as a rule, can take it. Or girls may misunderstand, and think that if something wouldn't bother them, then it won't bother a boy. A girl might not get upset about being called skinny? But to a boy, this might hold a completely different connotation. Skinny becomes scrawny in their minds, something that may bother them very much indeed.

But this book is written for you, so let's get back to the issue at hand, and that is boys and some of the issues you may face in this area through your eyes. I just ask that you remember that even though you may be dealing with some issues right now with the opposite sex, there are a lot of really great boys out there whose current actions may be clouded by the same pressures you are facing. And as always, remember that they deserve the same respect from you, that you (have the right to) demand from them.

TRUE or FALSE?

Boys naturally have higher self-esteem than girls … False.[1]

There is sometimes a misconception that boys don't struggle with self-esteem issues to the same degree as girls. This is not only wrong, but can be very harmful as their issues may be overlooked by others.

The Power They Have

From the time you were old enough to listen to your first fairy princess story, the power of boys was evident. They could swoop in to save you should you be caught in the claws of a fire-breathing dragon; they could rescue you from the isolation of a tall lonely tower; and their kiss is required to awaken you should you be cast into a spell-bound coma. Although it is not too likely in your current situation that you should require such services, boys still play a key role in a young girl's life and can exert a tremendous amount of influence over how you feel about yourself.

Their compliments can make you feel enchanted; their insults can sear your soul; and being unnoticed by them entirely can leave you feeling insignificant and invisible. And sometimes this all happens over the course of one relationship with the same guy! Whether you are actually dating or just exchanging covert glances across the lunchroom, this is the way it is with matters of the heart — dancing around your room one minute, crying into your pillow the next.

I mean it's not like this forever. Hopefully when you are older you will meet your prince and live happily ever after (if you want) — but that's another story for another time. We need to talk about right now. And right now, the truth is that many young girls at this age, girls just like you, suffer crushing blows to their self-esteem and make some fairly poor choices based on their desire to be the most beautiful princess in all the land loved by the handsomest of all the princes.

As I've mentioned before, this is not a magic book. Especially when it comes to this area, there is nothing that can save you from the highs and lows that will come from your first romantic interactions with boys. I'm so sorry, because, having gone through it myself (as all women have), there are going to be some pretty deep lows, so brace yourself! However, the bright side is there are also going to be some very great highs, so have fun riding that tide.

In the end, it will all settle out if you always remain, first and foremost, true to yourself and keep your eyes wide open. **When it comes to this area, understandably the heart rules and you can't always remain objective, but you don't have to turn your brain off either.** Just in case it does switch off once in a while, bookmark this page and refer to it whenever necessary. It doesn't contain any magic or special healing powers, just some simple tips, observations and encouragement based on the experiences of those who have been there.

You are not a princess, he is not a prince; you are not a vampire, he is not a wolf — you are a girl, he is a boy.

Romantic daydreams are great. They can fill many a boring class. But don't let your daydreams become confused with reality. If you want to be accepted for who you are, then you are going to have to offer the same in return. Sometimes girls get a little muddled here. It's easy to get lost in the daydream, to want the guy you like to be just like the hero of the latest blockbuster.

It is impossible to accept yourself, if you don't accept the reality of others. If you want the perfect boyfriend, then you are going to have to be the perfect girlfriend — and perfection, on any level, just doesn't exist.

And here is the point. If you accept another just the way he is, then you can allow yourself to accept yourself just the way you are. And that is the most important thing. Boys will come and go, but what you think of yourself will last a lifetime. So always be yourself and allow others to be themselves as well. If it doesn't work out because you didn't measure up to a boy's image of you, then too bad, so sad for him. Better to find this out sooner than later because trying to be something that you are not is not only exhausting, it's completely futile.

So always be yourself and allow others to be themselves as well. If it doesn't work out because you didn't measure up to a boy's image of you, then too bad, so sad for him.

You know how you look at all those pictures of girls on the magazines, commercials and MTV videos, and you think that this is what you are supposed to look like. Well, you are

All the boys in my class only like the blonde, skinny girls. None of the boys think I'm pretty.

— A

not the only one seeing those images. Young boys are also seeing those images and *some* of them are also buying into the hype and falseness of the images and thinking, "Okay, that is what my girlfriend is supposed to look like." This is especially true of younger or more immature boys who don't yet have confidence in themselves and so try to define themselves by their outward appearance (which includes the appearance of their girlfriends).

Boys like this will think that if they have that "image perfect" girlfriend then it reflects on who they are, like owning an expensive bike or a cool dog. These boys aren't necessarily shallow or bad, they are just falling into the same trap as many young girls. They are insecure so they grasp at what the media tells them they should like to help define themselves. The result, however, can be one more devastating blow to your self-esteem if you let it.

But take heart and stay true to yourself and strong in your self-esteem. It will pay off in the long run because eventually the boys worth being around will mature and become more confident. And as this happens, they trust themselves more and are attracted to girls based on their own decisions. The media images put before them won't influence them as much. They will see girls through their own eyes and want to be with girls who share their interests, their sense of humor or just have that intangible quality that makes their knees weak. And at this point a really cool thing happens — all that confidence you have built in yourself becomes a very attractive quality.

And these same boys, who were once so insecure, will find beauty in all shapes, sizes and types of girls. I know this for a fact, because, right now, all shapes, sizes and types of girls are in great relationships with great guys.

The heart wants what the heart wants. Who knows what attracts one person to another. Some girls love a boy with a short and stalky athletic build. Some girls like their guys tall and lean. Long hair, short hair, blonde, brunette, funny, musical, smart, poetic — the list of possible qualities one person can find attractive in another could go on for pages.

I don't find blonde guys attractive. Don't know why, just never have. It's no biggie.
— J

The point is that boys, just like girls, may be attracted to a certain *quality* in a girl. *Jessica doesn't gravitate towards blonde guys.* It doesn't mean that all blonde guys in the world are unattractive; it is just one person's preference. Remember this the next time a boy shows a preference. If a boy chooses to be with a specific girl because of the *image* he thinks it offers him, then he needs to do some growing up. But if a boy chooses always to date blonde girls because he finds blonde girls more attractive, then fine — no biggie.

It doesn't mean that you are not attractive just because a certain boy doesn't find you attractive. Don't let another's tastes define how you feel about yourself. They can't help it — the heart wants what the heart wants. The great

thing is that there are a lot of hearts in the world and they all want something different. So don't worry about being all things to every boy — be true to yourself and your beauty will shine.

The choices that you make in your life are yours to make. The compromises that you accept are yours to live with. But know what your choices are based on and know when you are making a compromise. Be honest with yourself and make sure that you can live with the consequences.

Sometimes a girl has such low self-esteem and so desperately wants a boy to like her, that she is willing to go to any lengths to attract him. This can be as insignificant as acting "girlie-girl stupid" to as destructive as compromising herself and her beliefs to please a guy. Not only can this put her in harm's way, it can lead to lifelong consequences, including undesired sexual encounters, unwanted pregnancies, a reputation

He said if I was willing to let him touch me "there" then I could be his girlfriend. I'm so excited because I really like him.

— S

that chases her, a photograph that follows her, a memory that haunts her.

And for what? Are you actually getting what you thought in the bargain? Occasionally when your self-esteem is low, you can confuse the attention a guy gives you for genuine like (or love). And just like confidence can attract, some guys can smell desperation from a mile away and it will attract the wrong kind of guy who is more likely to take advantage and leave you feeling worse than before.

The second that you have to act differently or offer something to a boy in exchange for their affection, warning bells should be going off. The second you do one thing in a relationship that you are uncomfortable with or makes you feel shameful, then stop! There is something wrong.

What choices you make from there are yours, but at the very least open your eyes to it. Is it really worth giving up all that you are going to give up? Will the consequences you have to live with, maybe for the rest of your life, be worth this one fleeting moment where you can pretend that a guy really liked you? And you will be pretending, because if a guy really likes you then all you have to be is yourself.

NOTE: If you haven't already done so, you may also want to check out "Number 5: But Sometimes Something Bad Is Just the Beginning and You Need to Cut and Run" on page 83.

When he called to break up with me, I could hear all of his friends laughing in the background. I can't believe that he could be so mean. I hate him!

— S

It's not you, it's me. We can still be friends. I thought I was over my old girlfriend, but I'm not. You're a great girl, but it's just not working. I think we need some space. It's over.

However it comes, whether through a gentle good-bye or a bitter bolt from left field, the end of a romance can be crushing. It's hard to imagine, if you have never gone through it, that something that once made you so happy could end with such sadness or bitterness or even hatred. Even if you are the one who initiates it, it can leave you feeling sad and maybe even second guessing your decision. And if you are not the one who wanted the break-up, it can leave you feeling much worse — mad, hurt, worthless, used, confused, embarrassed, ugly, unwanted or just plain sad.

Some may tell you not to worry about it because it was just *puppy love* and not real, but your feelings are real and the pain you are going through is very real. But if you open your heart to romance it is going to happen — and more than once. I personally don't know of one female who has not gone through some sort of break-up in her life. Unless you are Romeo

and Juliette (and we all know that didn't end well), it is very unlikely that your first love is going to be your true love forever.

The reason for this is pretty simple. You are young and new to this. You are still trying to figure out who you are, let alone what you want in a boyfriend. It can also be hard to know what another person is really like and how well you gel until you actually start spending time together. What you thought it would be like might not be what it is like. Plus, as you grow and mature you change, he changes, things change; what once worked might not anymore. There are lots of reasons why relationships end. Some may end better than others, but again, the odds are good that it is going to happen to you at some point.

Knowing that you are going to have to go through it doesn't make the "going through it" part any easier. There is nothing really that can be done to immediately take the sting out of heartbreak, but there are some strategies for easing the pain.

- *Balance Yourself.* Your heart might be broken, but your head is still working, so use it to balance your feelings. The sadness you are feeling should not be dismissed as unimportant, you are entitled to feel however you feel and take some time to get over it, but don't over-dramatize it because that will just prolong it and make you feel worse. Try to put it in perspective. "I'm sad right now, but my life is not over. I've got lots of good things going on in my life" or "I'm going to concentrate on getting lots of good things going in my life." With all pain in life there is a grieving period you may have to go through, but you have to want to work your way out of it by trying to stay as balanced as possible and keeping things in good perspective. If you embellish your feelings of heartbreak then you are only working against your own happiness.

- *Don't Dump on Yourself.* Even if your boyfriend was cruel in the way he broke up with you or the words he said, let that be a reflection on him, not on you. If you have been true to yourself and respectful of him then you have nothing to feel ashamed of, no matter what he says. This is why it is always important to be true to yourself, because at the end of the day the most important person you have to answer to is you. You don't have to be embarrassed or ashamed because you opened up to a guy who treated you badly. You didn't do anything wrong (except not have a crystal ball to tell you what the guy was like). If, like S, a guy is a total jerk and breaks up with you in a way intended to make you feel stupid,

it reveals what he is like, not what you are like. Always, always treat yourself and others with as much respect as possible so that you can always hold your head high. In life, you can only control your own actions, but if you are proud of your actions, then you will be amazed at what you can weather.

- *Pamper Yourself a Little.* You shouldn't wallow in your grief, but hey, everyone deserves a little pampering when they are down. This doesn't mean taking out a tub of ice cream (you don't want to fall into the trap of emotional eating), but something that makes you feel good, something a little special just for you like hanging with friends, cuddling up with a movie, painting your toenails, getting into that exercise program you were too busy to start, whatever works for you.

- *Know that This Is Normal!* That's my all-time favorite. I'm sorry, but it's true. I know that you might think that no one has felt the pain that you are feeling right now, and that is normal too. And all the things that you have heard are true — time does help heal and you can't actually die of a broken heart. You are amazing — good luck!

Sometimes prince charming doesn't look like prince charming at all. Sometimes the person we find ourselves attracted to might not match the cultural, religious or social expectations that we were raised with.

When this happens it can be very confusing and scary. You may feel ashamed or even mad at yourself for *allowing* yourself to become attracted to someone who may not be accepted by your family or social circle. This can be a hard issue to deal with for an adult, never mind a young girl.

If you find yourself in a situation in which your feelings are confusing or you fear may not be accepted by those around you, the situation will become much worse if you suffer in silence. If there is no adult with whom you feel comfortable approaching this topic, then there may be community help lines set up to discuss these issues with you. You do not have to be in crisis to call one of these hotlines, you just need to want to talk.

But please find someone trusted to talk to because some burdens are too heavy to carry alone.

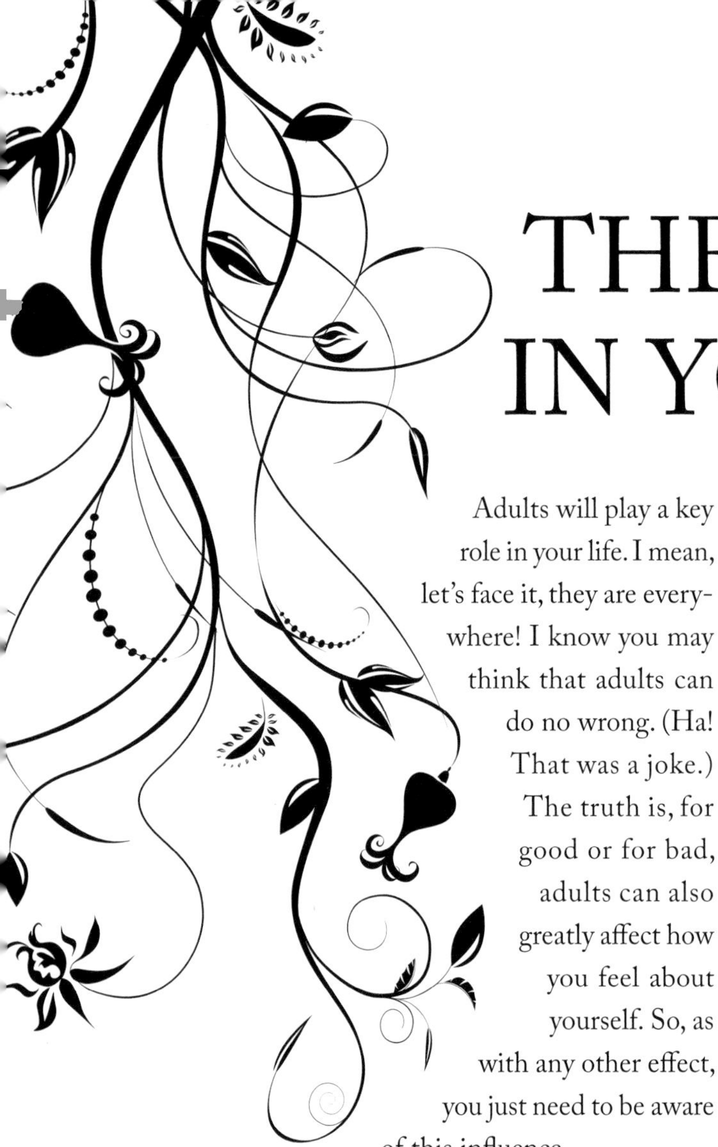

THE ADULTS IN YOUR LIFE

Adults will play a key role in your life. I mean, let's face it, they are everywhere! I know you may think that adults can do no wrong. (Ha! That was a joke.) The truth is, for good or for bad, adults can also greatly affect how you feel about yourself. So, as with any other effect, you just need to be aware of this influence.

1. *Adults Don't Always Get it Right.* No getting around the fact that adults have lived a lot longer than their young counterparts and therefore tend to have more experience and insight into many things (although I also know of children who have been through more in ten years than many adults will face in a lifetime). However, when it comes to their opinions of who you are and who you can be, adults don't always get it right.

   I only point this out because you are at an age when other peoples' opinions can influence you a lot. This is often more impactful when the opinion is coming from an adult. Just as a young person can rise to great heights because of the belief an adult has had in them, so too, can a young person's dreams and hopes, along with their self-esteem, be crushed by an adult who tells them they are no good at something or grades them below average.

   A *subjective* opinion about another's capability is just that — an opinion. There is no black and white or right or wrong when it comes to judging potential talent or worth. There are loads of examples of people (young and old, famous and not) who were told that their dream was unrealistic, their talent non-existent and their vision impractical — people who went on to great success and happiness following their dreams, talents and visions.

   Look it up the next time you become discouraged. You will find heaps of examples of famous scientists who failed at school, business leaders who got fired from jobs, artists who were told that their work just would not sell. Take, for example, the number of times that J.K. Rowling's manuscript for *Harry Potter* was rejected by people who just didn't think it was good enough. It's been reported that somewhere been nine and twelve publishers didn't see its value and rejected it. This is a book series that went on to sell in the hundreds of millions of copies worldwide — a series that may never have made it to print if the author had believed those first few people instead of herself.

Now, I am not advising that you never listen to anyone, or take their advice on how you may improve your opportunities. I am saying, however, (for example) if your passion is art, just because your eighth-grade art teacher gives you a bad grade doesn't mean you should give up on your dream or stop believing in yourself. Follow your passion through because that is really the only way that you are going to know for sure what you are capable of. And, if another, even an adult, ever tells you that you won't amount to anything, know that they are wrong because they don't have a clue what you can amount to as long as you believe in yourself.

2. *Adults Can Make Great Listeners.* Talk, talk, talk. Talking is one of the absolute best things you can do for yourself when you are faced with a problem or just generally feeling down

They Say the Darndest Things!

Hate to admit, but even we adults can say stupid things without thinking. Below is a small sampling of things I have heard directly or have been related to me by baffled parents.

- "You're so huge!" Said by an old friend of the mother's upon meeting, after some years, a girl suffering extremely low self-esteem over her height.
- "You look great. You've lost so much weight." Said by a friend of the family to a girl suffering with an eating disorder (a fact known by the friend).
- "Don't worry, they can do laser surgery when you are older." Said to a girl struggling with her looks after just getting glasses.
- "Don't worry, pretty girls don't need to be smart." An uncle awkwardly trying to comfort a girl embarrassed by her poor math grades.

So, the next time you are left reeling by a comment made by a supposedly intelligent adult, don't take it to heart. If it sounds dumb to you then it probably was dumb. It may be hard, but try not to let it get to you. (I find the best course of action is to stare blankly and then move away.)

about yourself. It is amazing the release that you get when you share your burden with a compassionate ear. And if you don't believe me, this is a zero risk proposition — just try it.

There are many great things about talking to a trusted adult.

- You know them and trust them and they honestly want the best for you. And if you don't know them personally, make sure that they are a trusted source (most countries or cities offer free, confidential, 24-hour help lines for kids in need). You have to be careful not to turn to anonymous sources, like those on the Internet. If you don't really know the person, often you have no idea who you are talking to, or what their motives are (and their motives might not be what is best for you). The point is you just don't know. I don't want to insert a bunch of scary stories here, but there are plenty of scary stories of kids getting mixed up with someone online who they thought was there to help them, but it turned out the opposite was true. So, be smart and find someone you can trust to talk to.
- It can be hard sometimes to talk to friends because they are often wrapped up with the same issues you are having. So a trusted adult can offer a balance and a perspective that just can't be found if you only talk to peers. It's someone looking in from the outside that may have a whole new and surprising viewpoint. Plus, in most cases, adults just have more experience. They have often been just where you are. And though the times may have changed, the fundamental issues are often the same. I bet you would be surprised if you asked your mom about how she felt at your age and how she coped.
- You may have gotten yourself into a situation in which you need help, or you might simply want someone who won't judge you, someone who will listen to you. In either case, allow those older folk around you a chance. They may surprise you.

FAMILY

Family, family, family — what to say about family?

Family can be the most wonderful supportive gift in the world or the cause of much grief, anger and frustration. The hardest part about family is that you don't get to choose them, but you have to live with them. Family relationships, for good or bad, can play a huge role in the development of your self-esteem.

Maybe you have parents who you feel don't understand you? Or maybe a brother or sister who you think is so much better than you? Or maybe you just don't feel like you can live up to what is expected of you? You are not alone. One in three girls with low self-esteem believe that they are not a good enough daughter.[2]

Whatever the issue, if you are having difficulty at home it can be particularly hard on your self-esteem, as home is the one place where you should be able to feel secure and most comfortable with yourself. You are not always going to get along with everyone in your family — you are all made up of unique personalities and opinions. But, overall, family is important to how you see yourself in the world and should not be ignored.

If you are feeling like you can't communicate or that you are not being heard or respected, then it might be as simple as telling those around you, calmly and respectfully, how you feel. Anger and yelling will never get you anywhere. Sometimes, people who live in such close contact take one another for granted and they don't even realize when they are hurting one another. You would be amazed at how much could be accomplished if you just sat down with your mom or dad and told them you how you feel.

However, if you feel that your situation is bigger than this, then you need to get some help. There are people who have a lot of experience and training who could help you — teachers, school counsellors, your family doctor, trusted relatives or kids' help lines are all a good place to start.

It can be incredibly devastating when you lack the support of those who are closest to you and improving things can take time, but don't give up on yourself or those you love.

What Did You Say?

Pride is a funny thing. On the one hand pride means self-respect — a good thing. But pride can also mean conceit and lead to stubbornness — not such a good thing.

Sometimes in relationships, especially family relationships, everyone is quick to blame others and no one wants to see their own role in the disagreement. Sometimes this happens simply because no one is actually listening to anyone else, so no one is even hearing what the other says. Everyone just assumes what they say is right and what the other person says is wrong. Everyone has been guilty of this at one time or another.

So a helpful hint, if you are going to put yourself out there and explain your feelings to another: it is important to listen to their response. After they have finished speaking, take a deep breath, pause for a moment and think about what they have said. This may not only calm you down if what they said angers you, but it also might change what would have otherwise been a hasty, unproductive comeback (a "wise-crack" as my dad would have said).

TECHNOLOGY, THE MEDIA & YOU

AND THE WORLD EXPANDS DESPITE OURSELVES

This "telephone" has too many short-comings to be seriously considered as a practical form of communication. The device is inherently of no value to us.

— Western Union internal memo, 1878

A rocket will never be able to leave the earth's atmosphere

— New York Times 1920

[Television] won't be able to hold on to any market it captures after the first six months. People will soon get tired of staring at a plywood box every night.

— Darryl F. Zanuck, head of 20th Century-Fox, 1946

This Room Is Equipped With

Edison Electric Light.

Do not attempt to light with match. Simply turn key on wall by the door.

The use of Electricity for lighting is in no way harmful to health, nor does it affect the soundness of sleep.

I know what you are thinking. *You know more about technology and media than me.* You're right. Indeed, every day the news has another story of a ten-year-old programming an app or a fifteen-year-old selling their software to Google. You most definitely know more than I about technology and social media.

But, thankfully, this section has nothing to do with learning how to use technology or setting up your profile on a social media site.

I know the next thing you are thinking. *I've heard it all before. They teach us all this Internet safety stuff in school.* Good, I hope you have heard a lot about that, because it's important stuff. But this section is not about Internet safety — how to protect your passwords or what information to give out on the net — all extremely important, but not the point of this book.

It's also not the point of this section to discuss if or how much you should be using all this stuff. That topic is a decision between you and your parents. I know toddlers who use YouTube and teens who still are not allowed to use cell phones. That's a personal decision.

The point of this section is to make sure that, like all things in your life, if you are going to be exposed to it, you keep your eyes open and understand the influence it can have on your attitude and your self-esteem. What your generation is being exposed to is relatively new territory. Experts can argue for days about the positive and the negative that has come from the availability of so much so fast. But, for our purpose, it doesn't matter. It's here.

The point of this section is to make sure that, like all things in your life, if you are going to be exposed to it, you keep your eyes open and understand the influence it can have on your attitude and your self-esteem.

THE PRESSURES AND PITFALLS OF POSTING YOUR LIFE

There used to be an old saying, "Don't write anything down that you wouldn't want everyone to see." The notion was that what you committed to paper could potentially fall into anyone's hands. Mostly though, this usually meant that your little brother might sneak around your room and get his hands on that diary you kept under your mattress. Sure it could provide a few moments of embarrassment, but it was not likely to end up being copied and handed out to everyone in your school. And if he repeated something, you could usually just accuse him of being a liar — not nice maybe, but effective.

Today the saying has been revised. "If you don't want it displayed in 20-foot letters on the gym wall during your school's spring assembly in front of every person that you know, including your parents and teachers, then don't write it." What you write now doesn't go in a diary, but rather to all your "friends" via social media sites, e-mail, texting or a thousand other ways in which your words are not hidden under your mattress, but rather sent directly out into the world. And not only words, but pictures too. Once this stuff is sent out into the world, you have completely lost control of it. But you know this already.

A picture you send to a boyfriend in confidence is soon being relayed to every cell phone throughout your school. A nasty comment that you made in the heat of the moment about a friend via text cannot be taken back because it lives forever to be shared with everyone in the group. The consequences become tenfold compared to the days of passing a note in class. It is near impossible for you to get that note back once it has left your keyboard.

But you are already aware of this. Fair enough.

So you may be asking, ***"If I know to be careful, watch what I post and what I say, what harm can it do?"*** It's not necessarily that it can do harm. I'm not suggesting that there is a boogie-man out there on the net just waiting to spring on you. But even the most careful user of social media might not fully realize a few of the subtle ways such interaction may affect their self-perceptions if they let it.

1. The Pressure to Be Perfect

According to fashion magazine, *Marie Claire*, the average woman spends three years of her lifetime "getting ready." Males may ask, "*Getting ready for what?*" Females don't require any clarification. We know what that means — the hair, the face, the clothes, then to the mirror, the self-criticism and back again to change the hair, the face, the clothes or maybe all three. And that is just for an average day, for a look that may last 12 hours and be seen by only a few.

So think about the added pressure when you have to come up with the all-important profile picture or countless lifestyle pictures that show the world how great your life is. I have heard of girls who take hundreds of pictures of themselves and then obsessively pour over them looking for just the right shot. Then they switch the pictures time and time again, putting an incredible amount of pressure on themselves to get just the perfect image. The one where they look pretty enough, or thin enough, or happy enough or cool enough. Do you recognize yourself here?

The issue here isn't that this process will probably double this generation's years of "getting ready" (although that is a pretty fantastic thought), but rather it's about the added pressure that you are putting on yourself without possibly even realizing it. Maybe you love taking a thousand shots of yourself and changing them daily — fair enough. As with all things though, just ask yourself this question: Are you having fun doing this or is it becoming hard to keep up the online image?

Because, unlike your real life, this universe has been developed of your own choosing and can be altered or shut down with the flick of a switch. Not that you have to shut it all down. You can still use all the social media you want, you can still be part of the conversation, but just go into it with your eyes open to the pitfalls and make sure that you are making the decisions that are best for you. You can choose to live on social media the same way you choose to live your real life. You can just be you.

2. The Over Exposure

It's not only the time investment in your posts that can leave you feeling a little overwhelmed, it is also the fact that you have opened yourself up to an entirely new forum, where anyone and everyone feels entitled to judge and report on your every move. People will say things through their keyboard that they would never say to you in person. **Very few people are going to come up to you in the school hall and give you a thumbs up or down on your outfit of the day**. On social media, however, it's as though you have asked to be rated. It is just the way it works. Sites are even set up with "like" and "comment" and "thumbs up and down" buttons to make it easier for people to casually judge you.

You might not realize it, but when you are constantly looking to others to validate what you say or do, it can undermine a lot of your confidence to just be you. Who wants to be critiqued 24/7? And it may not be right, but it's what happens. You know it. You post something and then people comment on it. You might say that it doesn't bother you, but are you very sure? It would take an incredibly strong person (like Hulk strong) not to be affected by at least some of it.

There is this rating site that all the girls in school have started using. You post a picture of yourself online and then people rate you from 1-10. I guess if you are super beautiful you want to go on so that everyone says how beautiful you are. But some of the boys think it is funny to rate the pretty girls really low just to mess with their heads. The whole thing is kind of screwed up.

— C

Now, unfortunately, some things make it to the wider world not through you, but because they are captured by a dozen different cell phones and posted by others. You may not even be aware sometimes that this is happening until you see it online for the first time yourself. And some of these things you may definitely not want to share with the world.

The only defense against this would be to never say or do anything in public that you don't want out there for all to see. But this is not very practical. I have not yet met the perfect person. If images of you get out there that you do not want seen, then first talk with someone who can help to get them taken down. It might be embarrassing to go to your parents or teachers, but trust that they are there to help you. If the damage is done, as they say, then you will have to find the strength in yourself and those around you, to deal with the situation.

This is why it is so important at this time in your life to lay a foundation of positive self-esteem and confidence. You will do stupid things in your life. Everyone will do stupid things in their lives. Unfortunately with all the available technology, some of those stupid things may be broadcast.

You have to believe in yourself and forgive yourself. Don't lose faith in yourself, don't cower in shame — you are amazing.

3. The Never-Endingness of It

There is nothing sweeter after a bad day, when you might be feeling particularly low about yourself, to leave it all behind and find a safe spot, under your blankets or in the arms of your dog, or buried in the pages of your favorite book. The world can be left at the doorstep for another day. Tonight is just about rebalancing and rejuvenating.

With the advent of social media, however, there is sometimes no end to the day. The dramas and feuds and anxieties of the day can follow you right through your door when you get home. So, it's important to know that you can turn if off if you want. You don't have to constantly be checking online to see if so and so is still mad at you. You don't need to fall asleep reviewing what the boys are saying about which girls are hot. You can leave it alone — that is your choice. And the thing about this is that this is another one of those super-easy tests you can try. The next time you are feeling a little bad about yourself, or just exhausted from all the drama, just turn it all off for the night and spend the time on yourself. See if it helps you put things back into perspective a little quicker.

I don't know a lot, but one thing that I do know is — it will all still be there tomorrow.

THREE QUICK WAYS TO FALL VICTIM TO THE INTERNET

I'm pretty much hoping that every kid, by the time they are old enough to type, has been taught about online safety. Never give out personal information; never meet someone privately that you met online; and so on, but this is not what this section is about. (Though that stuff is important so please make sure you know about it!)

Even if you know all your safety rules, you can still be greatly affected by the exposure you have to others online. One of the greatest things about the Internet is its ability to bring people together who might not normally have had the opportunity to meet. If you want to talk for hours about cheerleading, there are people out there who want to do that too. If you are struggling with issues of loss, there are online support communities ready to offer comfort. But beware because there are a lot of opinions out there and before you go looking you better be pretty sure of yourself. Once you are out there in the great wide world of the Web, it can be pretty easy to lose your footing and fall victim to someone else's notion of who you should be.

If you aren't really sure of yourself, if you have the least bit of insecurity about your looks, your preferences or your feelings, then instead of getting support from online communities you may, in reality, find yourself feeling worse or involved in a community that exploits your insecurities. And if you actually go out looking to find someone who will tell you that you are not good enough — guess what — it's not hard to find. If you have any insecurity and you want someone to validate it, then

For example, when researching this book I was online and came across a Web site hosted by a guy who was telling women what made a woman attractive to a man.

He didn't even have the good grace to say that this was just his opinion. He was actually stating his rules like they were facts. Thankfully, I'm secure (re: old) enough to know that this guy was a big fat loser!! I don't give a rat's patooty if he thinks women have to be a certain size and wear their hair a certain way. He might want me to believe that this is every guy's opinion, but it is not — it is his.

And then I clicked him shut, just like that.

Once you have found them, they can convince you that their opinions are the norm. That what they think, everyone thinks. That what they say is right.

you can find it. If you think that there is something wrong with you and you want someone to agree with you, they are just a click away, waiting for you.

And then, once you have found them, they can convince you that their opinions are the norm. That what they think, everyone thinks. That what they say is right. And herein lays the danger.

1. Believing It Is All True

For some reason the written word always seems so much more authoritative than the spoken one. Maybe this is because we have all been brought up to trust newspapers. Although you can't always believe what you read in a newspaper either, at least with newspapers, you know who wrote it. Someone is standing behind their words. You can assess the qualifications of the writer and decide if you want to trust their opinion. But this is not always the case on the Internet.

Take Wikipedia, for example. There is a reason why so many teachers won't let you use Wikipedia as a reference on a school paper. That is because we have all come to use Wikipedia as though it were the bible of all information. If Wikipedia says it, then it must be true. But the joke is on us. According to Wikipedia itself;

> Wikipedia is written collaboratively by largely anonymous Internet volunteers who write without pay. Anyone with Internet access can write and make changes to Wikipedia articles, except in limited cases where editing is restricted to prevent disruption or vandalism. Users can contribute anonymously, under a pseudonym, or, if they choose to, with their real identity.

So this means that anyone can write anything on any subject. They don't even have to use their real name when they contribute! In real life if, let's say, you were having a medical issue about which you had questions, you could go to see a doctor or you could walk up to some random person on the street and ask their opinion. Most intelligent people (which I know you are) would prefer the first option. You see, when you talk with someone in person you can put them in context and so you can put their opinion in context.

If Johnny, in math class, says that all blonde girls are stupid, well, you know Johnny. You can choose to listen to him if you want, but you will most likely put his opinion in context (Johnny is not that bright) and have an easier time disregarding it because what does Johnny know about it anyway.

But when something is written, when someone actually has a Web site or a blog, then it is easy to fall into the trap of thinking that they must *be* someone; they must have some authority on the subject. And if they write that *this is the way it should be*, then it can be very easy to fall into believing that *this is the way it should be!!*

But it's not. Unless it is a credible site that can actually be linked back to a credible organization, then the Internet is one big Wikipedia site — a bunch of people you don't know writing their opinions about a bunch of stuff. They may say the whole world is onboard with them, but just because they say it doesn't make it true; and just because they sound impressive, doesn't make their opinions any more important than yours.

2. Believing a Small Group Is the Whole World

One person's writings can make you second guess your own opinions if they are written authoritatively enough. Add to that a number of people who all share the same opinion, and then it can really shake your beliefs if you are not strong. There are over 7 billion people in the world, but just a few can come together into an online community and raise their voices like they represent the whole world.

Many online communities exist with a single focus. And they can bring so many arguments and so much pressure to conform that you can lose sight that this is just one small group within a group of 7 billion people. It can become very easy to accept that their opinion is the norm; that if you want to succeed you need to follow them.

It's kind of like that fast-talking car salesman often depicted in movies. He talks so fast and so much and so slick, that before you know it, you are buying a Ferrari, when you really just came into the dealership looking for directions.

When you encounter a group online that makes you feel like they are more than they are, then it is easy to lose perspective. If you have engaged in an online group that is promoting a certain way of life or telling you that you need to be a certain way to

A young girl's insecurity about her weight can easily be exploited on the Internet. Sadly, if you are obsessed with becoming super-thin and will go to any lengths to be as thin as possible, regardless of how much it hurts your body and mind, then it is very unlikely that anything you read here will change your mind. No matter how many times you are told you are beautiful just the way you are, no matter how many times you are told not to value yourself by superficial standards, no matter how many times you are told you are so much more than a number on a scale, it won't matter because you have to believe it yourself. The respect you have for yourself has to come from within you.

And for as many positive messages you get, you will receive negative messages, if you are open to them. A boy may call you fat, a friend may make an insensitive comment, but don't blame others. If you choose to hurt yourself for the sake of thinness, then own it. You can walk away from negative comments; you can disregard ridiculous images of half-starved, obsessed girls who are just as afraid as you about not fitting in. You can choose to put yourself first.

But if you want to find support for making yourself miserable and sick over the shape of your body, then there's lots of that around. You don't have to look far; it's just a click away. The Internet is full of sites dedicated to supporting a girl's quest for ultra-thinness, regardless of how unhealthy it may be. These sites will offer you tips on how to achieve your goal. They will congratulate you on the pounds you lose. They will tell you that you are strong and successful for not giving into temptation. You will become a part of a club — you will fit in. Lucky you!

What these groups won't do is ask how you are feeling; they won't care if you are sick and miserable. They don't want to know anything about you. They don't care how you lose the weight, just as long as you lose it. They just want you to be like them. They *need* you to be like them so they can convince themselves that they are somehow right and good and strong.

Strength is a big message from many of these groups. They will tell you that you are strong and in control because you can resist temptation at any cost. But this is not strength. Depriving yourself of the basic food you need to live does not come from strength, it come from weakness. It comes from low self-esteem. It comes from the fear that someone might say that you are not good enough, because you are not thin enough. It comes from a place of fear and insecurity, not strength.

Don't fall victim!

succeed, look outside this group. Rebalance yourself. Speak with people in your own life who you trust about the messages you are being given. Get lots of opinions, but in the end, trust yourself. You usually know deep down what is right for you and what is not. Don't be bowled over by others. You have a choice.

3. Assuming the Motives of Others Are Always Good

There is no other way to say this than simply: Sometimes people just want to stir it up. Don't assume that everything you read exists because the person writing it really believes it or because they want the best for those who read it. Sometimes, just like in real life, people just want to get a reaction from others. The trouble with the Internet is that a lot of it is anonymous and therefore people will write things that they would never have the guts to say in public. Sometimes they do it for a joke, sometimes they like to get people upset, sometimes there is no understandable reason.

There have been documented instances where someone online encourages another to self-harm. They pretend they are a friend, a supporter, but they are actually just playing on the other's insecurities for their own amusement. This is a sad fact of life. I wish it were not so. But it is, so don't fall victim to it.

Remember, for the most part, those you come across on-line are strangers. They don't know you and you don't know them. If you acknowledge this, then you will be in a better position to protect yourself from someone else's harmful opinions when you are vulnerable.

IT ALL LEAVES A MARK

Pretty much everything you interact with leaves a mark. Songs you listen to. Video games you play. Television shows you watch. Books you read.

Let's look at a typical scenario. You cuddle up after a good day with your favorite reality program, *Drama on Drury Lane.* The key characters, Mindy and Belinda, are at it again. They are supposed to be BFFs, but really, Mindy is going after Belinda's boyfriend behind her back. And to make matters worse, Mindy has just lied and told Charlotte and Tina that Belinda was the one who stole Charlotte's wallet at the party last night, even though you know that it was Tina who lost it, but Tina is now afraid to say anything. *Cut to scene.* Belinda is screaming at Mindy, Charlotte is trying to wrestle Belinda to the ground, Tina is cowering in the corner crying ... and commercial.

This used to be the action you would see on soap operas — made up TV shows where actors played the parts. Soap operas have given way to reality TV — some would say made up TV shows where non-actors play the parts. The difference here is that regardless of whether the drama is real or not, you are told that it is real. You are expected to think that this is real life.

So, you've had a great day. Now to complete your day, just before you lay your head to sleep, you cuddle up with *Drama on Drury Lane* — a supposed real life account of how others spent their day. They are yelling and screaming and rolling around on the ground. In general, they're behaving just short of how a pit of rabid dogs would interact.

How does this make you feel? Maybe you think it is funny because you know how stupid it is and you find it entertaining. Maybe it depresses you to think that other people would actually interact like this. Maybe you don't think about it at all. And that is the point. Everything you interact with leaves a mark. It might be a tiny mark or it might be invisible, but there is a mark and it can affect how you feel about yourself.

People's reaction to what they are exposed to varies. Different people are affected in different ways. Many times people aren't even aware of the effects because they never ask themselves the question or relate their feelings to what they saw or read. **It's like when a dog eats a plant and an hour later is throwing up. He can't put it together that it was because it was that plant he ate an hour before. So he goes out and eats the same plant again the next day.**

You may know when you watch a really sad movie that you are going to feel sad. Or, if you are brave enough to even watch it, that you will be checking your closets for a month after watching the latest *Halloween* horror flick. But that is not what we are talking about here.

It's when you watch, read or listen to something over and over and over again, that, at first, doesn't seem to bear any relation at all to the way you feel. These *hidden* effects are the ones you really have to watch for. But the very fact that these are *hidden* is what makes them so hard to decipher, especially when so many things can impact you on any given day.

So as with all things, you need to keep your eyes open and your brain on. And keep asking yourself questions. Questions about how you feel after watching or seeing something. Questions are a fantastic way to get yourself thinking. Discussion is another great tool. Ask your mom, or friend or brother what they think of your favorite TV show or music. It is an interesting way to view things from another perspective, which also might get you thinking of things you never thought of before.

Constant Criticism

What's more fun than seeing a celebrity blasted on the front cover of a magazine for being too fat? Some magazines even go so far as printing photographs of the women (it is almost always females) and then circling in red any signs of cellulite (fat).

Or how about when they track a celebrity and report on every bit of weight gain? Or how about the TV shows where celebrities are critiqued on their hair, makeup and clothes in scathing detail? All pretty funny right?

On the one hand, it's normal to take some glee in the fact that these celebrities, who are often presented to the world only when done up by professional stylists, are finally shown to look like real people. But is that the only mark these types of magazines and shows are leaving on you?

Maybe. Or maybe, without even realizing it, the message you are getting is that it is okay to laugh at someone because you don't like their outfit, or shame someone who has gained weight, or make fun of a new haircut, or expose someone for having cellulite? Initially you make think this is okay because they are celebrities and they somehow deserve it, but the message is the same. It's okay to judge and ridicule someone based on their looks.

And what kind of mark may this leave on you? If you read or watch these magazines or TV shows all the time, in which women are constantly being ridiculed for something like their weight, then the message you are supporting is that superficial qualities, like weight, are really, really important to how someone is valued. When you see enough of this stuff, how can you not help but to start looking a little closer at yourself in the mirror to see how you compare?

Distorted Images of Reality

The average amount of money spent on a wedding dress in the United States is $1,100.[1] You may not believe this if you are a devoted fan of one of the gazillion wedding shows that regularly promote the idea that you need to spend at least $5,000, preferably $10,000, on a wedding dress if you really want to be happy.

There are a lot of incredibly strong and successful girls and women throughout the world who have done a tremendous amount towards advocating for and celebrating the beauty and strength of girls and women worldwide. You might not believe this if your world consists of reality shows that expose you to the idea that women spend all their money obsessing about the way they look, and all their time fighting and backstabbing the other women in their life.

There are a lot of guys out there who want to be with a girl because she makes him laugh, because they share an interest, or because he likes the way she cares more about the competition than her looks when playing soccer. There can be a million different things a guy finds attractive in a girl. You might not know this if all the videos you watch only show girls as being attractive to a guy when they are half-dressed and adoringly fawning all over him.

There are a lot of diverse girls in the world. You might not remember this if all the programs you watch only show you the same type of girl over and over again.

There is just a whole lot of life out there that isn't anything like what you may be seeing or hearing or reading in the media.

You might think because it is mindless, it is harmless. That's not necessarily so. Just like all those images you see on the billboards, one or two might not affect you much, but through repeated exposure it can add up to a great impact. Unless you can see the unreality of it all, you might not even realize the mark that it is leaving.

I go on a canoe trip every year with my family and family friends. There are usually at least eight kids on the trip — boys and girls. It is my absolute favorite trip of the year. I would rather be there than anywhere.

We go into the bush where there is no washroom or running water. We bathe in the lake and generally stay in the same clothes most of the trip. We run around the forest for days, playing capture the flag and whatever. No cell phones or anything work in the bush so there is no contact with the world. I love that. You are so cut off from everything, it is so relaxing and freeing.

You kind of forget about any problems.

— K

CAUTION: DANGER AHEAD

I wish that you never felt bad about yourself. I wish that you could always see yourself in the mirror the way that you truly are — as a beautiful, strong, and valuable young woman. I wish that you made only the best choices for yourself in life — choices that made you strong and reaffirmed the amazing person that you are.

But it is not likely that this will always happen. Sometimes, we all get off course or make choices because we feel sad or mad or insecure or worthless or lost. Or sometimes the choices we make are because we are impatient and want to speed up a goal we have. Or maybe we are making a conscious choice of how we want to live without fully thinking through all of the consequences.

This chapter is not about telling you exactly what choices you should make in life. That would be impossible. Sometimes the only way to find out if something is good for you is through trial and error. Harsh but true.

But there are a few areas where those who have gone before can share some of their experiences and hopefully give you a little insight and save you a little pain.

FAT FIXATION

FAT. The most dreaded of all three-letter words. This tiny word has so much power that it can bring a grown woman to tears and leave even the most confident girl a quivering mess should it be uttered against her. There seems to be no greater insult to hurl at a female than this. Call me stupid, call me mean, call me rude, insensitive, ugly, conceited, call me anything — just don't call me *fat*.

In fact, when speaking to young girls it is advised by some professionals that the word *fat* is not even mentioned. As though the word itself holds so much evil power that just the mere mention of it might be incredibly damaging to a young girl.

But it is *just* a word. When it is directed as an insult, it is a very hurtful word. There are a lot of words that can be hurtful if you let them.

"Fat" is *just* a word. And not mentioning the word is not going to keep the insecurities you have around this subject from swirling in your head or the anxieties over it from rising in your throat.

The power that we, as females, have allowed this word is mind-boggling, especially given two facts.

1. Every layperson's definition of fat is different (I can't tell you how many times I have heard a beautiful young girl honestly complain of being fat when it is just not true).
2. The relationship between a girl's weight and her beauty is in the eye of the beholder, and the relationship between her weight and her intelligence, spirit or value is completely non-existent.

Do you know what it is like to always feel fat?

When I was in grade seven a guy I had sort of liked for a while made a joke one day when a bunch of us were fooling around after school. We had started a pick-up game of football, and one of the guys said that he wanted me on his team because I could plow over any of the guys.

It took everything that I had to keep it together and pretend that his stupid joke didn't bother me. My eyes were literally stinging with the tears I was holding back. I was embarrassed not only because he said it in front of other guys, but also in front of my girlfriends. They stood up for me and said he was a jerk, but honestly that just made the whole thing worse — like I was some kind of freak who needed to be protected.

I swore from that day on to just stop eating. And if I couldn't stop eating then I would get rid of everything that I put in my mouth by throwing it up. I didn't really know what I was doing, but I vowed that I would do whatever it took to get skinny so that no one could ever hurt me like that again. That is all I focused on.

It's a really long story, but I can tell you this. This idea isn't what it's cracked up to be. I treated myself like crap, I felt like crap, I always felt like I was failing because either way I had screwed myself. Either I was not losing weight and so I felt like I was a loser or I was losing weight but I felt generally bad and tired and I was mad and sad all of the time. And then it became a whole huge thing with my parents when they saw what was going on. I don't even want to go into that. The whole thing just got out of control.

In the end I know I was also mad at myself for being so weak that it mattered that much to me about what other people thought of my looks. Like that is the only thing I counted for. I was willing to do anything, hurt myself and my family, just so some guy would say that I was skinny. How pathetic was that?

— W

Fat matters when it is directly related to your health. Too much or too little of it can pose serious health risks and even death.

The self-perception of fat matters when it affects your self-esteem. I say "self-perception" because there are plenty of females in the world who are healthy and are perfectly happy and confident in their size despite the fact that they may actually be considered *fat* by some people.

The Fat Facts

Here is some information you might want to keep in mind. There won't be a test.

- There is no perfect weight or body shape that will guarantee perfect happiness, love and success.
- There is no perfect weight or body shape that will make everyone in the world think you are beautiful. Physical beauty is in the eye of the beholder, and as discussed throughout this book many times, everyone has a different eye.

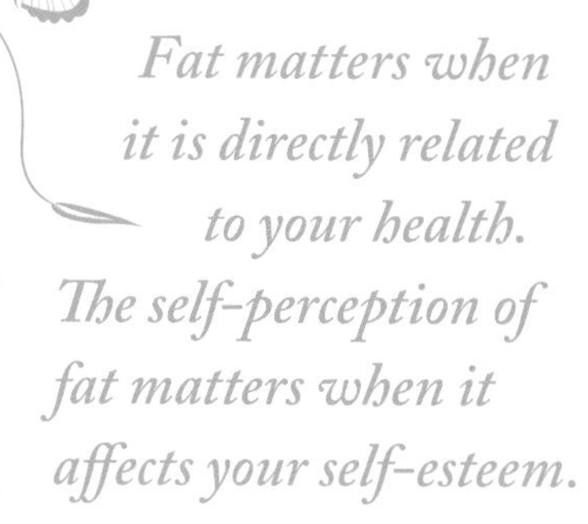

Fat matters when it is directly related to your health. The self-perception of fat matters when it affects your self-esteem.

- There is no perfect weight or body shape that will make you strong inside. Strength comes from within you, not because of what you look like on the outside. There are plenty of unhappy size 0 girls in the world hurting because of their insecurities.
- If you let the *word* have power over you, it will have power over you no matter how much you weigh. *Fat* is just a word. If it is spewed in insult, it exposes the ignorance and smallness of the speaker and takes away nothing from your beauty or strength.

The Danger of Diet Pills

What they promise seems too good to be true and that is because it usually is.

Diet pills may offer a magic solution, but the truth is most are ineffective and diet and exercise is required for any noticeable change. Not only is this an expensive option, but it can also be a dangerous one as this is mostly an unregulated industry. Among many of the reported side effects of such pills are liver damage, increased blood pressure and heart rate, stomach pain, nausea, gas, headaches, mood changes and the list goes on.

And just because it says "natural" on the label doesn't mean it's good for you. Snake venom is also natural! Be smart and don't fall for the advertising. Don't start taking any diet supplement without checking with your doctor first — your real doctor, not someone on the Internet who says they're a doctor.

- This might not make you happy, but it is a fact. Genetics and body frame do play a role in both your weight and body shape. The statement, "I have big bones" is true. Not every girl of equal height will be able to achieve naturally equal weight or body profile. Maybe not fair, but there are a thousand things that aren't fair when it comes to genetics. You will live a much more peaceful life if you accept that now.
- Healthy diet and proper exercise will make you feel much better about yourself in the long run than starving yourself skinny.

If you are obsessed about your weight to the point where it is causing major depression, anxiety or self-harming behavior, then please let someone know because you need some extra support right now to help you. And that is okay. A strong person knows when to get help from others. You are a strong girl.

If you feel you need to reach a healthier weight, the best way to do this is through proper eating and exercise. This method is also known as the good, old-fashioned way. It takes time and effort, but will build healthy habits for a lifetime.

If you are thinking of experimenting with some shortcuts to weight loss because it is cool, or all the other girls are doing it, or you are not patient enough to do it the good old-fashioned way or because the good old-fashioned way won't yield the results you want, then consider the following when choosing your direction.

Anorexia = Refusal to eat. Sure you lose the weight, but there are some other potential side effects that you might not find as sexy.[1]

- ☠ Heart problems
- ☠ Kidney failure
- ☠ Seizures
- ☠ Menstruation stops
- ☠ Muscles waste away
- ☠ Bowel problems/ constipation
- ☠ Weakness
- ☠ Bone loss
- ☠ Depression
- ☠ Hair loss
- ☠ Bloating
- ☠ Dry blotchy skin
- ☠ Death

Bulimia = Trying to get rid of all the food you consumed in an unhealthy way (e.g., vomiting, using diuretics, excessively exercising, any method of purging all calories). You get all of the above potential side effects, plus a few others.[2]

- ☠ Damaged and discolored teeth
- ☠ Sores in the throat and mouth
- ☠ Sores, scars or calluses on the knuckles or hands
- ☠ Chipmunk cheeks/swollen cheeks
- ☠ If you use laxatives to make you poop instead of vomiting away your food, your body can become so dependent on them that you won't be able to go to the bathroom normally anymore.

Eating disorder behaviors can become addictive so don't risk it.

Fat doesn't make you less. Thin doesn't make you more. Taking care of yourself, being proud of who you are and being the best that you can be makes you everything. Please believe me and everyone else who tells you that you are more than a number on the scale or a size on a pair of jeans. **You need to understand this now or this issue will haunt you for the rest of your life and cloud every aspect of who you are.** Be part of a generation to stand up against this incredible stupidity. It's a waste of time, money and emotion.

It started in grade six for the first time. All the girls in class just stopped eating at lunch. It was the thing to do. I think a couple of the popular girls started it first and then it was like, "It's not cool to eat. You'll get fat." So most of the girls barely eat anything at lunch now.

I guess it got pretty noticeable because some of the teachers started making us show them what we had eaten, but it's not hard to lie about that. I'm not exactly thin, but my weight has never bothered me, so I just go along with it and then pig out when I get home. But I think it is becoming a problem for a couple of the other girls.

— R

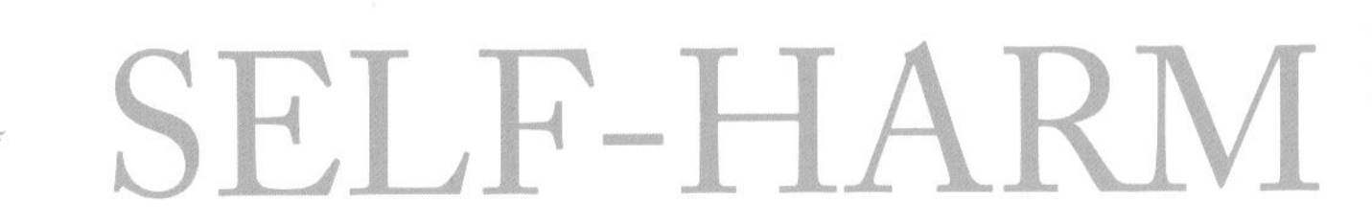

SELF-HARM

Self-harm refers to the act of deliberately harming your own body. Anytime you try to hurt yourself on purpose, whether through cutting your skin, taking toxic substances or in any other way, you are self-harming. There are a lot of different reasons that people may self-harm.

Feelings of anger, sadness, guilt or anxiety that can lead you to want to hurt yourself need to be taken seriously. If you are feeling beyond despair, like you have no choice but to hurt yourself, if you feel like you deserve to be hurt or if you think the pain will somehow make you feel better, then *please, please get help.* You have nothing to be ashamed of. Don't hide your pain from your friends or family because they are there to help you. You will never know how good life can be unless you give yourself a chance, but you need to let someone know first so that they can help you.

Self-injury, also called self-harm, is the act of deliberately harming your own body, such as cutting or burning yourself. It's typically not meant as a suicide attempt. Rather, self-injury is an unhealthy way to cope with emotional pain, intense anger and frustration. While self-injury may bring a momentary sense of calm and a release of tension, it's usually followed by guilt and shame and the return of painful emotions.[3]

If, however, you are contemplating experimenting with self-harming behavior, like cutting, because someone is pressuring you or has convinced you that this is a cool thing to try, or because all the other girls are trying it, pause and think. There are serious consequences to this behavior even if you are not taking it that seriously.

- Cutting can become habit forming, which means that the more you engage in this behavior, the harder it will be to stop. You may lose control of this without even realizing it.
- Even if you think what you are using to cut with is clean, you can develop serious, gross infections from cutting from the very first time you try it.
- Cutting can result in permanent scars or disfigurement from the very first time you try it.
- Any self-harming behavior can result in serious, unintended medical consequences or even death from the very first time you try it.
- Cutting and self-harm can lead to overwhelming feelings of shame and guilt from the very first time you try it.

Don't risk it. And if you know of anyone else who is experimenting with this behavior you *must* tell someone. Even if they become angry with you, even if they tell you they have it all under control, even if you risk losing their friendship — you have to tell someone because they are risking their life *from the very first time they try it.*

I couldn't really tell you why I tried it. I was just really angry. It had been a really crappy week and I was mad. All my friends had been real jerks and my parents kept saying, "Don't worry about it." I was mad at my friends, I was mad at my parents and I thought that it would make me feel better. One of the girls at school had told us that she did it, so I thought, "What the hell."

I knew right away that I had made a mistake. When my parents found out, it became a huge thing and even though I told them it was a one-time mistake, they watch me a little differently now. I'm so embarrassed. I really don't want people to label me "a cutter."

— E

Teen and young adult females are at the greatest risk to self-harm. Any number of mental and social issues can contribute to the decision to self-harm, but girls at risk can also be influenced by their friends. Girls who have friends who intentionally harm themselves are more likely to begin self-injuring.[4]

JEALOUSY AND ENVY

Although these words are often used interchangeably, there is actually a subtle difference between being jealous and being envious.

Jealousy tends to refer to the feeling that you have for another when you fear that you may lose something because of them. *You are jealous of the new girl at school because she has become friends with your best friend, who is now spending time with her instead of you.*

Envy more often describes a feeling you may have when you want something that someone else has. *You are envious of the new girl at school because she is taller and thinner than you and you wished you looked more like her.*

- Both feelings are completely normal to a point. We have all felt jealous or envious of another at some time in our lives.
- Both feelings can actually influence positive change, if managed properly.
- But both feelings can also result in very negative outcomes if not handled right.
- And (good news), both feelings can be controlled.

The first thing to realize is that you are not a horrible person just because you feel jealous or envious of another. So don't beat yourself up. The important thing is in how you handle these feelings. That is what you will be judged by — both by yourself and others. It is important to get these feelings under control, because they often do you more harm than the person they are directed against. No one likes to feel jealous or envious of another. It's just not a good feeling.

Many times emotions of jealousy or envy are related to your own self-image or self-esteem issues. They are rooted in your own insecurities. This is why, as with so much in life, the more you work on your own self-esteem and confidence the easier it will be to deal with what life throws at you.

Sometimes, though, you can be completely confident and still experience these feelings.

For example, if you lost the lead in the school play, you may become jealous of the girl who did get it. In this case, you might have been completely confident in your ability to perform the lead part and feel jealous because this other girl got in your way. No self-esteem issues here, just good, old-fashioned anger.

What to do when you feel jealous or envious?

1. The first thing you have to do is be honest with yourself about your feelings. People are often very embarrassed to admit that they are jealous or envious because they feel it shows a weakness in them. The good thing is that you only have to admit it to yourself. (You can whisper it to yourself very quietly. No one else need know.)
2. Once you admit it, you then have to figure out exactly why you are feeling what you are feeling. It's hard to handle a problem if you don't understand why it is happening. Luckily though this is usually pretty easy to figure out if you are honest with yourself. It can be embarrassing to admit why you are feeling this way, but again, this is a private matter between you and yourself. Don't try to fool yourself because you will know.
3. Once you admit to your feelings and to the reasons for them, you can do something about it. **And this is the important step because this is where things can go relatively good or horribly wrong, depending on how you choose to handle the situation.**

Let's look at a couple of typical situations you might come across and explore a few ways you might handle them.

You are jealous of the girl picked, over you, for the lead in the school play.

- Focus all of your energies on blaming this girl until it completely consumes you and makes you feel sick inside.
- See only the negative in the situation so that you make yourself as miserable as possible.
- Complain to everyone you know that you have been "ripped off" and that the other girl "stinks" until everyone is sick of hearing about it and you look like a completely bitter drama queen.

OR

- Allow yourself to feel sorry for you for a very short period of time (go home and treat yourself to something).
- Realize that it is not the girl's fault. She did not make the casting decision.
- You can just let it go. You are not always going to get what you want. Move on to Plan B.
- If you still want to be involved in the school play, find another place for yourself in the play, either onstage or backstage.

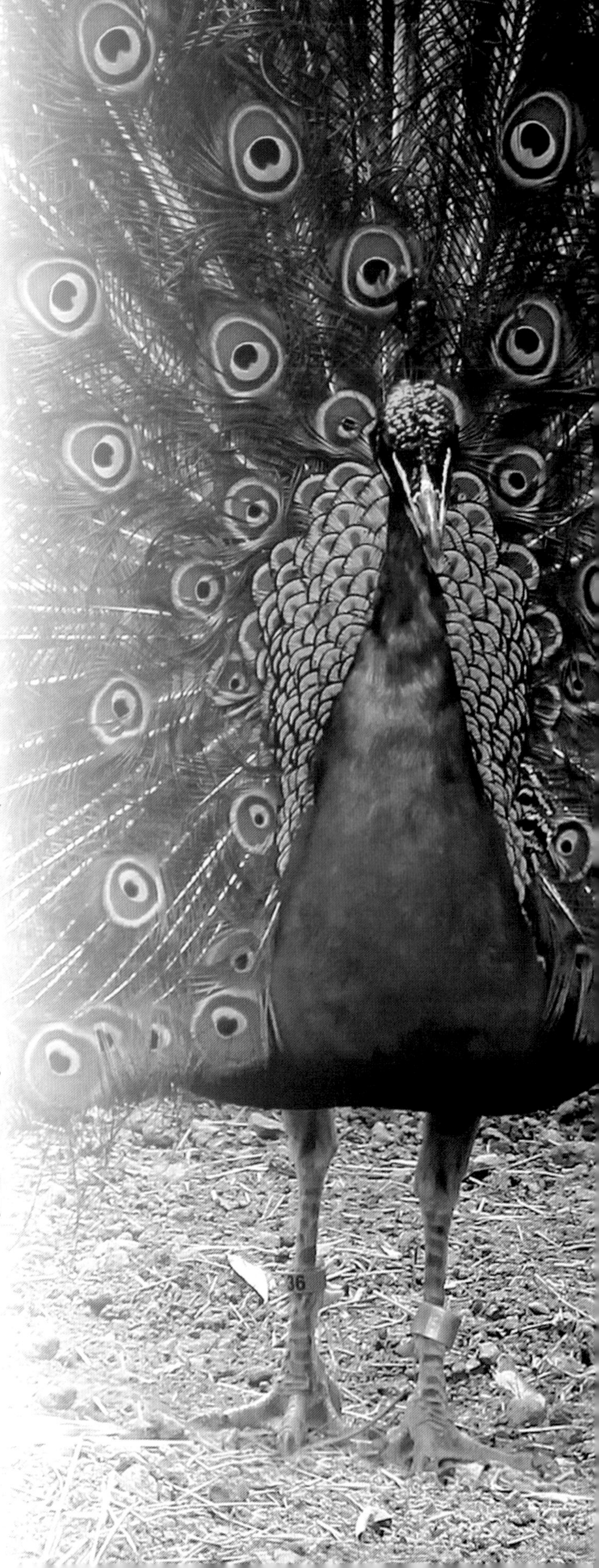

- Use the experience as a learning opportunity. Talk to the teacher who did the casting and ask what she based her decision on and how you can improve your next audition.
- Put things in perspective and rebalance yourself and your priorities. This might not have worked exactly like you wanted, but there are lots of other opportunities.
- Take the high road and offer the girl good luck in her role. You will feel amazing.

You are jealous of the new girl at school because she has become friends with your best friend, who is now spending time with her instead of you.

- Keep all of your feelings bottled up and stew with anger until you hate both the new girl and your (former) best friend.
- Confront your best friend in a very negative manner, yelling at her and telling her what a rotten friend she is until she is yelling right back at you.
- Strike out aggressively at the new girl and/or your friend (e.g., fighting, spreading rumors, etc.).
- Blame yourself. Allow your insecurities to grab hold of you until you convince yourself that it is your fault that your friend doesn't want to hang with you because you are somehow not good enough.

OR

- Pause and take a breath.
- Let your friend know how you feel. Do you know how many relationships have been screwed up because one person expects the other person to be a mind reader?! You may not always get the answer you want, but at least you won't be wondering. Plus, it is only fair to the other person who may have no idea why you are upset. *Talk, Talk, Talk* — can't say that enough.
- Okay, so if you have talked it out, hopefully it has all worked out (and the three of you are friends forever), but, if the communicating doesn't yield the outcome you hoped for:
  - Put the situation in perspective and don't blame yourself. Relationships change (see Friends, Frienemies and Foes). This is not necessarily anyone's fault. Or maybe it is. Maybe your friend is just not treating you nicely (again, see the Friends chapter). Or maybe you have learned something about yourself. Perhaps there is a reason that your former friend doesn't want to hang with you anymore. (The catch is that when you communicate your feelings to another, you have to listen to their answers — it's part of the bargain. You might not like their answers, but keep an open mind. This could end up being one more of those annoying learning experiences.)
- Once you face the situation head on, it will be easier to move past the jealousy and just deal with the situation.

You are envious of the new girl at school because she is taller and thinner than you and you wished you looked more like her.

When you envy what another person possesses, it can be harder to resolve the feelings within you because feelings of envy come from discontent within yourself. They are not the "fault" of the other person. If you are not happy with the way you look and you are envious of another's appearance, you won't suddenly like your looks just because the other person disappears. You will still be discontented and you will just become envious of someone else (and there are a million someone elses out there).

This is not to say that some good can't come out of envy if you do it right. Sometimes envy can lead to a positive change in you. For example, if you envy the talent another has on the piano or the grades another gets in math class, that may motivate you to try harder to emulate those achievements. A great way to turn a situation around is to use others to inspire you. You may never achieve their greatness in a particular field, but you will be so proud of yourself for reaching that it may surprise you how quickly the envy melts away.

Other times what you envy you just can't achieve. You may never be as thin as your best friend. You may never be as tall as you would like. You may not be able to afford that horse ranch that *she* has. You may never be able to run the ten-minute mile no matter how hard you train.

This is life. And things you envy one minute will change the next minute if you are always looking outward instead of inward. Until you are happy with yourself, you will never be satisfied. You might think that you can't control these feelings, but you can. You just have to choose to — for real. No one said it would be easy, but it is your choice and your choice holds a lot of power.

Left unchecked, jealousy and envy can lead to lifelong behaviors that can destroy you inside and jeopardize your friendships.

ATTENTION-SEEKING BEHAVIOR

This behavior usually isn't that hard to spot. The kid telling jokes in the middle of class, pulling faces behind the teacher's back, lobbing spit balls across the aisle, coughing loudly, snorting loudly, doing everything loudly. He or she might just as well be wearing a huge sign across their chest — look at me, *look at me, Look at Me!*

There are a gazillion types of attention-seeking behaviors and just as many reasons why someone might use them — some justified, some not so much.

Sometimes you may experiment with this kind of behavior without thinking it through. And sometimes the result you get is not at all what you intended.

> *My friend Janie got mad that her boyfriend wasn't paying attention to her anymore so she scratched herself all up and told everyone she was cutting. She just wanted her boyfriend to feel sorry for her but he just got mad.*
>
> — S

At this age you can mistake the success of getting an immediate result with the success of actually dealing with an issue. When you just look for the instant payoff, you might run into a whole heap of trouble that you never saw coming.

Sometimes you *have* to stand up and say, "Look at me. Pay attention to me." But it is the way in which you do it that you have to watch. Problems can arise when you look for a quick fix and will do anything to get it, even if it means completely abandoning who you really are. If you try to be something that you are not just to get attention, it can backfire, sometimes horribly.

- You dress a certain way to attract a boy's attention. It works, but what he assumes you are looking for is not what you are looking for at all. You just wanted him to think you were pretty, but he thought that you were putting out sexual signals and were willing to do things that you are not.
- You hurt yourself for some quick sympathy, but things go a little further than you intended and you actually really hurt yourself by mistake.

It is not hard to get a boy's attention if you really want it. Just slap on some makeup, push-up bra, a low-cut top, short skirt and some high heels — and bango-presto, you are all of a sudden the bell of the ball.

— B

There are any number of things that can happen that you might not have planned for.

- Suddenly you have a reputation or a label that you can't shake.
- You put yourself in an unsafe situation and are in over your head before you even know it.
- More than just the people you wanted to know find out, and now you have to deal with your parents, and teachers and counselors who are worried about you.
- You are left feeling embarrassed or stupid and worse than before.
- It doesn't actually deal with the core of the issue. You may have gotten the attention you needed for a quick fix this time, but what about the next time? The issue is still there.

You are not always going to be happy, but you might actually end up making yourself more miserable if you don't stop and think before you react.

Deal with the real issue. Understand what the real issue is, whether it is insecurity in yourself because boys don't seem to notice you, anger because someone is treating you badly or whatever. Be honest first. Then look yourself in the mirror and remind yourself what an incredible young woman you are. Then stand up for yourself and ask yourself, "Do you want to approach the situation with honesty and dignity or are you willing to disrespect yourself to get a quick reaction?" The choice is yours.

Remember, when you deal with a situation, if you treat yourself with respect and are true to who you are, then you are in a better position to deal with any consequences.

For example, let's say that you like to dress in short skirts and a boy gets the wrong idea. If you have confidence in your choices and you are making them because they are what you want, not to catch someone else's eye, then you will be in a better position to handle the situation. You will be confident enough to tell the boy to "take a hike" if you don't like his attitude. And even if others don't agree, at least you can honestly say that you behaved in a way that you are proud of, so you don't have to feel ashamed of yourself or of other people's reactions.

PEOPLE PLEASING

From the time of your very first playdate, these words have been engrained in you — *Be Nice*. And they have probably echoed through your life ever since — *Be Nice*.

Yes, the world could definitely do with a little more *nice*. Offering your support and assistance to others will not only help them, but reap the added benefit of making you feel really good about yourself. And this is a good thing. But it has to be balanced. When you are nice to others you should never have to sacrifice your own feelings or beliefs.

Nice isn't always what it's cracked up to be.

Being nice should never leave you feeling bad about yourself. If you do for others, or allow others to do to you, because you think that this is what is expected of you or it is the only way that people will like you, then this is not a good kind of nice. Not only will it increase your feelings of worthlessness (maybe without you even realizing it), but it can also potentially put you into some bad situations.

All of these actions could be described as nice.

- Paying for everything when you go out with a friend.
- Going along with the crowd.
- Not making a fuss when you are the butt of the jokes.
- Taking the blame for a friend when something happens.
- Being there *whenever* a friend calls.

These all sound like pretty nice things. And they might be or they might not be. It all depends on everyone's motives and the balance in the relationship.

Sometimes a friend may be down on their luck a bit, and you paying for an outing is a really generous act that helps them out of their tough time. Sometimes you need to put others first and compromise. Sometimes, it is important in life to keep a sense of humor and laugh at yourself. Sometimes a friend has made an honest mistake, and you can step forward, without the same consequences, to help them out. And sometimes a long-lost friend really needs your support right now.

Or, maybe the only way that you are ever invited to come along is if you pay. Perhaps going with what the crowd wants means doing something that you are really uncomfortable with, dangerous or illegal. Probably you do have a good sense of humor, but the jokes are constant and mean-spirited and only entertain the one making them. Possibly, a friend threatens you if you don't take the blame for something they did. And maybe the only time this

person calls you is when no one else is available and they never think of you otherwise.

Same actions; different realities. Be honest about the difference.

As always, open your eyes and look honestly at the situation. What are your motives and how are you treating yourself. Have you convinced yourself that you are only being nice, when in reality you are doing whatever others want because you think it is the only way you will fit in?

Are the people you care so much about pleasing respecting you back? Do you feel good after you have spent time with them, or used, ashamed or worthless?

Most everybody wants to be liked by others. This is completely normal. But if someone wants to be with you only when you are offering them something (even if that something is just quiet submission), then you have to ask yourself, "What is the point?" You are getting to spend time with this person or group of people, maybe even the coolest crowd in school, but you aren't really gaining any real friends. And in the process you may be so completely disrespecting yourself that not even hanging with the cool crowd can make you feel good about yourself.

It has been said a lot throughout this book, but it remains true in so many situations. You have to be true to yourself and you have to respect yourself first so that you can demand that respect from others.

All good friendships require compromise once in a while, but it is okay to say "No" too. It is okay not to do what everyone else wants, if it is not right for you. Don't let anyone make you feel bad about that because if you can't respect yourself, you can never feel good about yourself. It may be hard in the short term. You may have to stand alone, but in the long run it will be so worth it.

Be nice to others *and* to yourself!

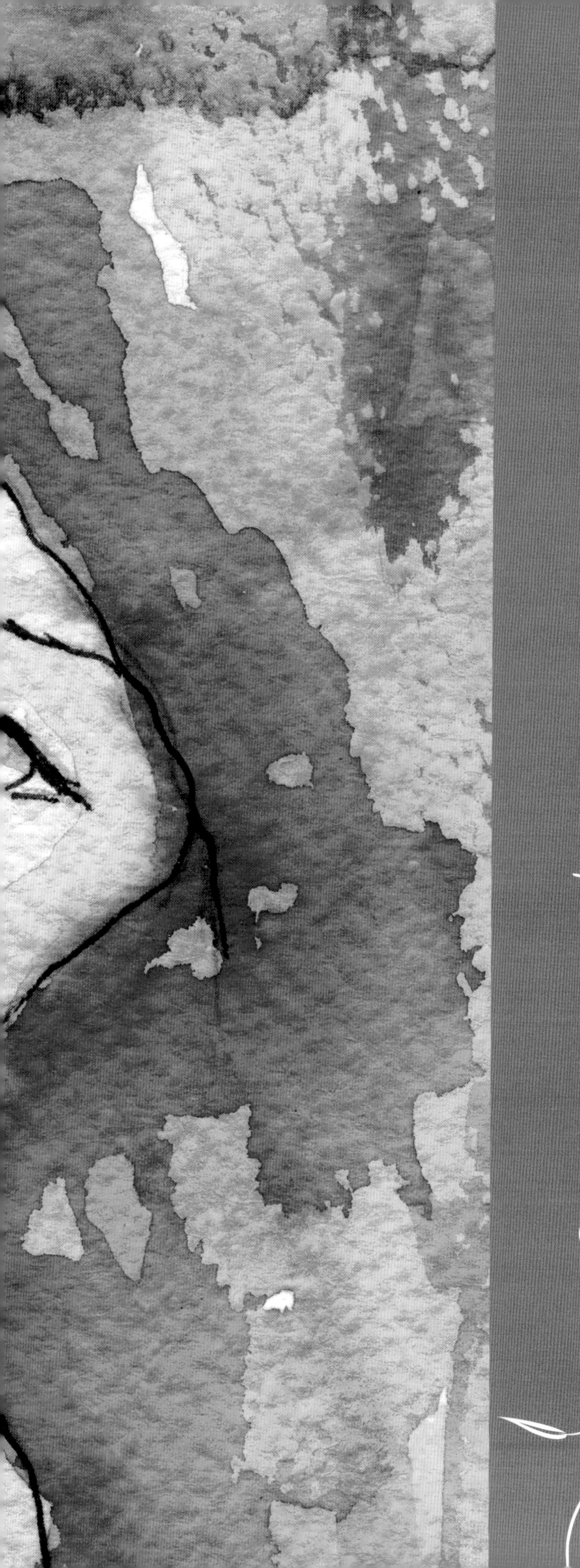

THERE IS A LIGHT

It might be hard to believe when you feel like the most unattractive, awkward girl in the world, but there is a light at the end of the tunnel.

It might be hard to believe when you are so embarrassed by something that you never want to leave your room again, but it won't always feel this bad.

When you feel sad, angry, lonely, stupid or invisible, remember that things will get better.

And when you feel like you just don't measure up to everyone else, know that you do and that you have the power within yourself, right now, to start seeing yourself as the truly amazing girl that you are.

It won't come easy. You will have to do all the hard work yourself. But you can do it.

Just being aware of the influences around you can make a big difference to how you see yourself in the world. And while there are no magic spells that can make you feel great about yourself all of the time, the following are a few thoughts that might help you along your way to realizing what a super, fantastic, amazing girl you really are.

The world is lucky to have you — now you just have to realize that yourself!

NOTE: You might think that some of these ideas are lame or too obvious to make a difference, but, like with most things in life, you may benefit if you just keep an open mind. You would be amazed at how a small effort can make a big difference. Plus, they are free for the trying, so what have you got to lose?

TAKE CARE OF WHAT MOTHER NATURE GAVE YOU

One of the quickest fast tracks to feeling better about yourself is to take care of yourself physically. I know, I know, you may hate your body and just want to hide it away, but the minute you start investing some time in taking care of it, you will immediately begin to have a more positive attitude both about yourself and about all the craziness around you.

Exercise and eating right is key to taking care of yourself. And I'm not talking about some boring, rigorous routine designed to make you lose as much weight as possible. Exercise and eating right is not about losing weight; it is about making your body as strong as it can be. I know I said that there were no magic spells in this book, but this one comes pretty close, **because a really amazing thing happens when you spend your time positively investing in your body instead of fighting against it**.

As your body becomes stronger, so does your mind, and your confidence and your ability to face life's challenges in a positive way. I'm not saying that a lifelong dedication to activity is going to make you always love your body, but you will have a much happier (and healthier) relationship with it and the world around you — for sure!

Move that Butt!

In addition to the benefit of maximizing how you look, exercise has many other benefits too.

- Boosts your energy level, so it helps you out in lots of other areas of your life as well. For example, the next time someone says something mean to you, you will have the energy to walk or jog away.
- Releases a whole bunch of chemicals in your brain that naturally make you feel better about yourself. (This is science stuff, but it is true.)
- Reduces your stress level. Next time you have a tough day, dance around for half an hour to your favorite tunes. The music and the movement are a wonder cure and you are so busy working up a sweat, you just don't have time to fret about the latest drama at school.

- It can be done for free. No money, no problem. You don't need a fancy sports club and you don't have to belong to an expensive team. You just have to want to do it.
- It's fun. Or at least it should be. Exercise can be anything that you want it to be to get your body moving — dancing, swimming, skateboarding, whatever. You can do it with a group or you can do it on your own. It's all about you and what makes you happy. This is an area where there is no one judging, comparing or grading you. It's for you, by you.
- You never know where it might lead. As you make peace with your body, you might discover a whole range of hidden talents that you never knew you had. Being so tall might just mean that you are a star at track and field. Or you might just feel free and confident enough now to pursue that love of dancing. Or getting out and jogging might cross your path with that really cute boy down the street. Who knows, life is funny that way!

The Stuff You Eat

There are about a billion books out there about healthy eating and every one of them I am sure could speak better on this topic than I can. I know, for example, that if the food is packaged and has a shelf life of forever, then it probably isn't that great for you. I know that eating a bag of chips before bed will play havoc on my waistline, my complexion and my mood. But I couldn't explain all the specifics as to why.

I do know that there are a lot of opinions out there as to what constitutes healthy eating; some I agree with, some not so much. Some of it is common sense, and some of it may surprise you. For example, I just assumed that anything that said *granola* on the cover must be healthy. It turns out this is not true!

So, while you will have to turn to more qualified help than I can offer for all the ins and outs of proper eating, let me start you off by throwing out a couple of things you can think about in the meantime.

- *Whacky diets and fads are whack.* While these gimmicks may get you some short-term results, they are impossible to sustain over a lifetime, and may actually contribute to weight gain over the long run. Also, depending on the diet, it can be dangerous. Such extremes will offer no lasting affects in terms of your self-esteem and confidence because the change won't be lasting. Put in the work, put in the time, change your habits and take care of yourself if you really want to see a positive change. The rest is just smoke and mirrors.
- *Think about the drinks.* Man oh man, you want to talk about marketing genius, then let's talk about the *ice-capped frappucino mochacino whateveracino latte drinks* or the *banana mango a ton of other fruits that the average person has never even heard of whipped yogurt smoothie*. Dessert shops and coffee shops did a really brilliant thing with these types of drinks.

  "Watching your weight? Don't want a milkshake — no problem. Have a real fruit smoothie instead. Don't worry about the calories — it's fruit!"

  "Skipping dessert? Not going to pay $5 for that piece of cake? No problem. Just have one of our lattes instead! (By the way, that'll be $5)."

  I have literally seen girls who refuse to eat a decent meal suck back one of these gazillion-calorie drinks without a second thought. The notion that if it comes in liquid form then it doesn't really count is misplaced.

A lot of these drinks are like hoovering melted dessert. Now, this is not about telling you what you should or shouldn't eat — that is your choice. But you should understand what you are putting in your mouth so that you can make an informed decision. When you buy something from a restaurant or coffee shop you have the right to ask exactly what is in it and what its numbers are (how much sugar, calories, etc.). If you ask, they should happily provide this information for you (in most places it's the law). If they don't, then take your business elsewhere (they need you more than you need them).

- *And speaking of marketing-related food genius, how about those super-charged energy drinks (and chocolate bars and powders and liquid shots)?* Although often more targeted to boys, these are another example of how the food industry has done an amazing job of getting us onboard with a new product without us ever questioning its benefits or possible side effects. All the slick advertising and sponsorships of cool events has quickly equated these types of drinks as the "go to" beverage for the hip and daring.

  What is not advertised is that one serving of many of these drinks have more than twice the daily recommended dose of caffeine, which can be not only addictive, but can leave you feeling nervous and irritable. Not great, especially if you are already feeling nervous and irritable about other stuff.

  NOTE: Nothing to do with self-esteem, but worth knowing. Excessive caffeine can also raise your heartbeat, so depending on how much of this stuff you drink in combination with your level of activity, it can also potentially be dangerous.
- *Emotional eating will destroy your self-esteem.* A tub of ice cream when you are sad, a bag of cookies when you are bored — we've all done it. And you are going to do it too. An emotional meltdown once in a while is human. An ongoing dependence on food to get you through your troubled times, however, will just add to your troubled times.

  Unlike, for example, a good cry that can really flush out the old system and leave you feeling tired but somehow relieved, eating a lot of junk when you are upset will just leave you feeling heavy, uncomfortable and probably even a little ashamed. There is really no upside to gorging your way through a rough patch. In fact, it will most likely make you feel worse about yourself in the long run.

MIND OVER MATTER

Whether you want to call it spunk, determination, spirit, moxie, energy or any of a dozen other names that describe that elusive, intangible quality that makes a person take charge of their own life, you have it and you can choose to use it to feel good about yourself.

If you don't think that you have it or that you have the choice to use it, you're wrong.

You already know that you have a huge ability to make yourself feel a certain way because you often use that ability to make yourself feel bad.

Well, you can flip that around and use your energy to work on making yourself feel good too.

This is not easy, which is why a lot of people don't even bother trying. In fact, this is probably the hardest of all the suggestions, but it also has one of the biggest paybacks. And even though some will find this challenge too hard, it can be done — you can do it. It takes commitment and practice — the commitment is to practicing it every day.

- You have the **choice** to listen each and every day to how you talk to yourself. To consciously make a mental note of the types of messages you are feeding yourself.
- You have the **power** to practice talking positively to yourself. Work each day at giving yourself a positive message about who you are. Maybe there is one small thing that you like about yourself physically, like let's say, your nose. Fine, remind yourself every day what a great nose you have. Or maybe you are really proud of yourself for making the track team. Great, remind yourself every day what an accomplishment this is.

This will have a tremendous effect, not only because you are being positive, but because it leaves less time for being negative. Eventually, you will find more and more positive things to say about yourself, because you really are amazing, you just have to spend the time discovering it.

- You have the **choice** to lose all the guilt and shame you feel because you don't look like some imaginary image of perfection or because you don't measure up to someone else's idea of beauty or worth.
- You have the **power** to allow yourself to just be you. Think about it. You can actually let go of all that pressure that you put on yourself every day, just like that — poof! You can choose to accept who you are. You can spend your energy dealing with the world around you instead of on your own personal self-waged war. You are going to have to fight enough battles in life, why add to them by fighting against yourself?

Developing the ability to think positively about yourself is a greater gift than any physical attribute you could possess. You might not understand this now, but know that it is true. How else can we explain that the world includes a lot of sad, insecure girls *with seemingly perfect bodies and glowing complexions*? The joy you get from life will not come from the size of your jeans; it will come from within you.

MAXIMIZE YOUR ASSETS

You may not love them, but your assets are what you have and if you actually accept yourself and work with what you have, instead of desperately trying to fulfill someone else's ideal, you will be amazed at how good you can feel.

Here are a few thoughts which may be helpful.

Not every fashion looks good on every body. This doesn't mean that there are good bodies and bad bodies. Every body can look great, just not necessarily all in the same thing.

For example, I am relatively short. I have tried year after dismal year to wear one of those long flowing peasant skirts that always look so elegant and hip in the magazines. I go to the store. I try one on. I look like I have just been swallowed by a leaf bag, and then I buy the skirt. I go home. I put it on. I look like I have just been swallowed by a leaf bag. Then I put it in the abyss at the back of my closet not to be seen again. Why do I go through this ritual, when I know it just won't work on me? Probably because every spring the latest fashion mags come out with some beautiful girl in a long flowing peasant skirt dancing around a meadow. (You might get better at accepting yourself as you get older, but that doesn't mean that you can't still fall for a few of the same old traps.)

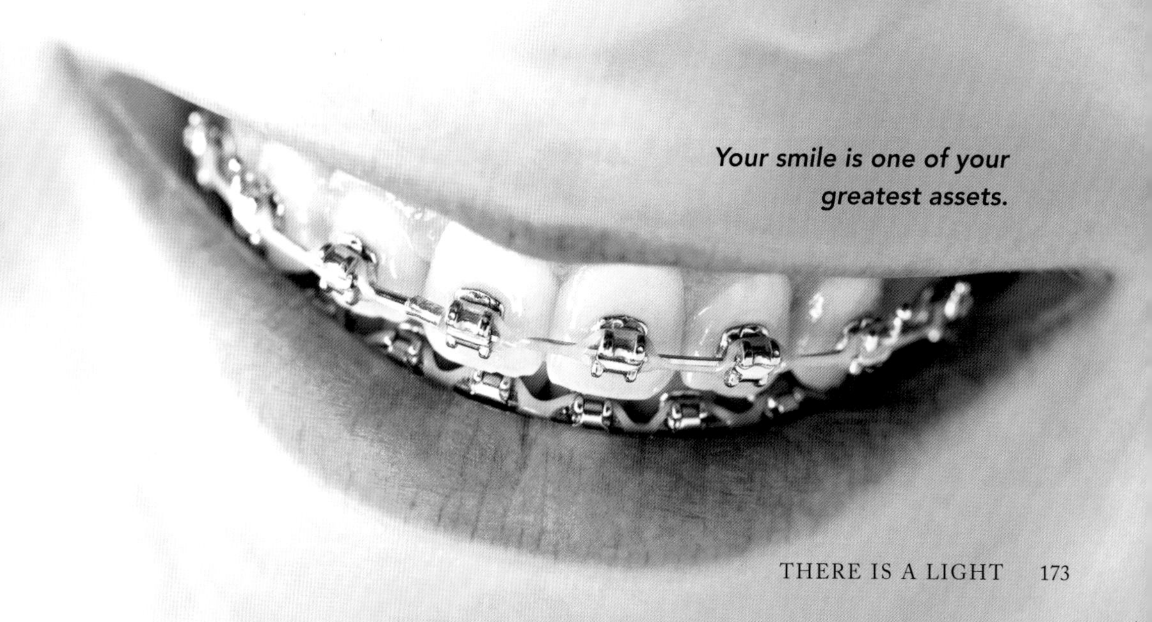

Your smile is one of your greatest assets.

The point is, lots of things look great on me — just not long, flowing peasant skirts. So, the moral of the story is *move on*. Too many girls make themselves feel bad by stuffing themselves into the fashions that they think they *should be* wearing, instead of dressing for the body they actually have. Rather than feeling good when they look in the mirror, they feel depressed and frustrated with the image that stares back at them. You know if a fashion is not working on you if you feel this way when you look in the mirror. If you are not overjoyed when you see yourself in the fitting room mirror, then it will only get worse when you get home. (I've wasted a lot of money not following that rule.)

There are enough different styles of clothes out there that you will be able to find what speaks to you, but only if you are courageous enough to look. I say courageous on purpose, because it does take a lot of courage to stand apart from the trends and dress only for yourself.

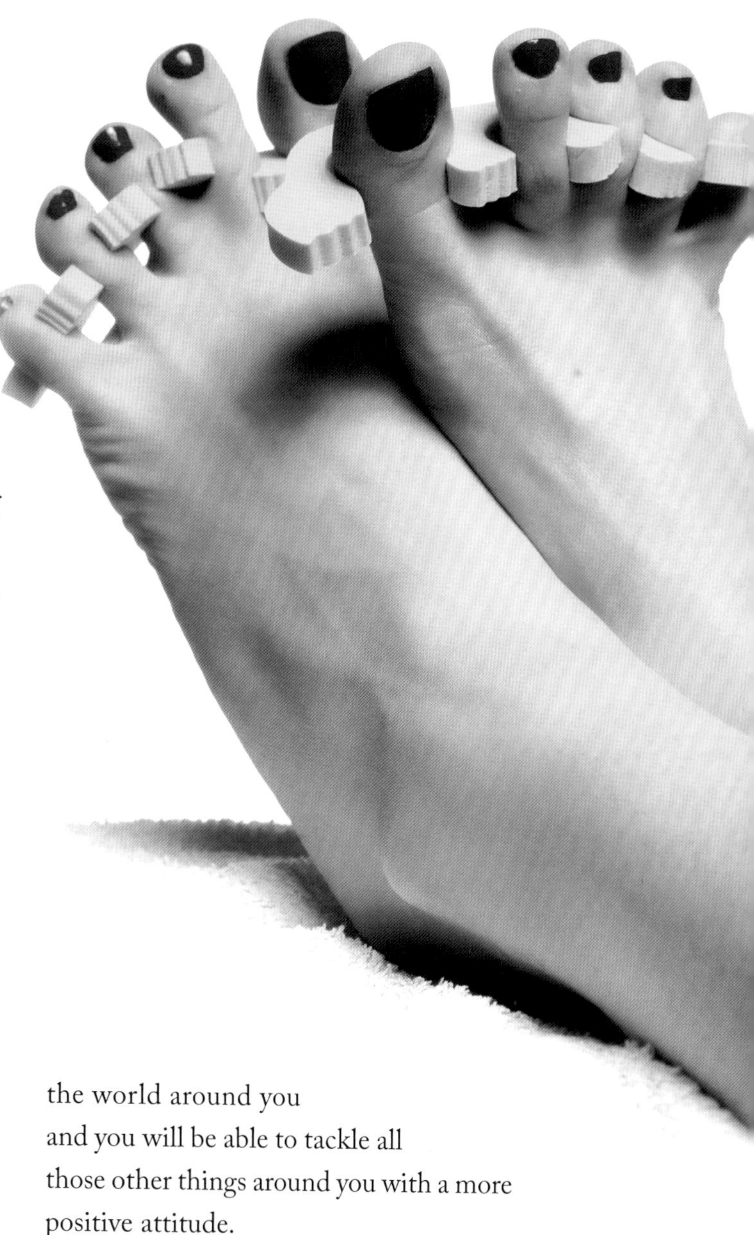

Don't let your self-esteem be ruled by your wallet or the labels on your clothes. It's easy to fall into the trap that you have to wear a certain label or shop in a certain store in order to be considered cool or accepted by people. This can be particularly damaging to your feelings of worth if you cannot always afford such things.

If your friends define you by the label you are wearing, then, really, what kind of friends are these? (That was a rhetorical question, meaning you don't really have to answer it because we all know the answer.)

With most everything we have talked about, how you spend your money is your choice. The purpose here is just to remind you to keep your eyes wide open. The next time you are in a store straining to figure out how to pay for that *must-have* labeled sweatshirt you so desperately want, just understand what is going on. There are a thousand sweatshirts out there, understand why you need this one. If it is just to buy into the image, then at least be honest with yourself so that you are not so disappointed when your wallet is empty and you realize that this sweatshirt didn't change your life like you hoped it would.

Have fun with it. There is nothing wrong with taking the time to make yourself look and feel good. It is not a waste of time and it is not vain to take time over your appearance. If you take the time to care for yourself, you will feel better about yourself and the world around you and you will be able to tackle all those other things around you with a more positive attitude.

This is, however, different than becoming obsessed over your appearance. There is a critical line between wanting to take care of your appearance and spending all of your time fixing, worrying, changing and generally being consumed with the way you look. The first is taking a positive interest in looking your best; the second is using a negative eye to judge yourself. The second is a waste of time and self-defeating.

There are lots of things that you might not be able to change about yourself, but that doesn't mean that you can't play with what you have. For example, as I may have mentioned, I have not been blessed with the gift of height. I could fret that I am not 5'9", like all the models I see, or I can put on a pair of heels when I go out at night and feel like a whole new person. It is not that I need to change myself, it is just that it is fun sometimes to try new looks. (Don't even ask me how many different colors my hair has been!)

There are lots of fun things that you can do to play with your appearance. This could be as simple as practicing good hygiene (I don't feel alive until I am showered and clean) to more specific treatments like plucking your eyebrows, trying new fashions, dying your hair, curling your hair, etc. The trick to making this work for you is that you have to make changes with a positive attitude and only for yourself. Don't try to change yourself to fit someone else's mold and don't become discouraged because you can't get your hair to look just like someone else's. Ultimately you will look amazing if, and only if, you wear it with confidence.

! Make sure that you get the experienced help you need when attempting certain beauty treatments. I have heard plenty of horror stories of girls who have completely plucked off their eyebrows because they didn't know what they were doing! Oh yes, and I may say the choice is yours but the reality is it is really probably yours and your parents. So please don't do anything without permission and then try and blame me.

More than 55 million cosmetic surgery procedures will be performed in 2015, predicts a recent study in *Plastic and Reconstructive Surgery®*, the official medical journal of the American Society of Plastic Surgeons (ASPS).

Cosmetic surgery is the act of altering your physical appearance through the use of medical intervention. This could be through surgical or non-surgical procedures and can result in permanent or short-term alterations. For example, I can surgically and permanently change what my nose looks like or I can non-surgically and temporarily get rid of wrinkles through special injections.

Often times when people think of cosmetic surgery, the immediate thought is, "That is soooo vain." This is not true. Many cosmetic surgeons have done amazing things to help people who have suffered trauma or been born with debilitating birth defects. The issue here is not with the medical specialty in and of itself. As with so many things in life, the issue of cosmetic surgery is a large and complex one and needs to be considered in relation to the motives and objectives of each individual case.

Now, if contemplating a cosmetic procedure, this is not likely a decision you will be making alone, if for no other reason than they are usually very expensive and require parental consent. So if it actually gets down to it, you should have lots of good guidance.

But when thinking of this now, or more likely in the future, consider it, as with all things in your life, with honesty and with your eyes wide open. Unlike dying your hair, the effects of this decision, both physically and mentally, can be lasting, so you just want to make sure that you truly, truly understand your motives for desiring such an extreme procedure and ensure that your expectations about the results are grounded in reality.

DON'T IGNORE THE GOOD

My son used to do this thing when he was little that I would like to share with you.

He could be having the best day ever. It could be like Christmas and he got every present that he asked for and then he got to eat as much cake and ice cream as he wanted and then clowns dropped out of the sky and gave him more presents and then just for good measure, the Easter Bunny showed up and gave him a magic machine that never ran out of candy. In other words, overall, a pretty good day. But then, just as he was getting into bed, he might accidently bump his head and all of a sudden, declare very loudly, "This is the Worst Day Ever!"

The funny thing is that this way of looking at the world is not unique. A lot of people, even as they grow, continue to focus more on the negative than the positive. This is not fair — to yourself or the world around you.

Here is something you can try for yourself. At the end of each week, before you catalogue in your mind the bad things that happened, think hard to come up with the good things that happened (the positive feedback, the good test score, the laugh you had with a friend, the goal you reached in track, the painting you finished, the compliment you got on your new outfit, etc.). At first, these moments might seem small and insignificant to you, but if they are positive they count, no matter how small, because that is the other unfairness — ***a bad can seem big no matter how small it is, but a good has to be huge before we even acknowledge it.***

The more you practice this way of looking at the world, the more positive your outlook will be overall.

And it is not just the things that happen to you that you should take the time to notice. Really open your eyes to the world around you and don't simply see what you are expecting to see.

My daughter has an issue with her size. She thinks that she is ugly because she is not as thin as some of her friends.

So I am watching MTV with her the other night and there are a lot of beautiful, sexy, gorgeous women on screen who are nowhere near the size 0 that she desires. But when I ask her what she thinks of some of these women, she says they look great. She doesn't even notice the size of their thighs, or the curves they have.

She is seeing exactly what she is expecting to see on MTV — beautiful women. She is not actually seeing that they have bodies just like her. It is so frustrating.

— Pam — a mom

BE STRONG

When you are feeling bad about yourself, it is easy to just give in, to just feel sorry for yourself and assume that there is nothing you can do about it, to think, "They're right. I am stupid or ugly or worthless." Feeling sorry for yourself is not hard. What is hard, what is incredibly hard, is standing up and believing in yourself despite all the messages you might be getting to the contrary.

If you think that this is just a meaningless *rah-rah* speech, you are half right. It is a *rah-rah* speech, but it is not meaningless. This is your life, whether you love it or hate it right now; it is the one you are dealing with. So you can just give up and spend the next years feeling bad about yourself, or you can make some hard decisions and decide to do something about it. There will be a lot of hard decisions, decisions to stand alone when you need to, to reach out when you should, to practice every day being more supportive to yourself, to ignore the naysayers and to embrace all that you are.

There are a lot of different ways that you can look at the world that will help you embrace yourself, but ultimately no book, no word of advice, no magic spell can do it for you. You will have to do it for yourself. But you are so worth it, so at least give it a try.

Being strong doesn't mean you have to do it all on your own. Strength also comes from asking for help when you need it. Never struggle in silence because there might be a solution right there for the taking if you just let someone know.

Middle school was really weird for me. On the one hand, I loved all the friends I had there and all the activities. I was on the volleyball team and in the school play, and that part was great. But I was never good with the actual work.

Math was the worst. No matter how much I tried, I could never get a really good mark in math. The days we got tests back were the absolute worst. I was always so embarrassed when everyone started comparing marks because mine for sure was going to be one of the lowest. Eventually I just assumed that I must just be stupider than everyone else. And then I just tried to play it off, like, "Yeah, what an airhead girl I am!"

But even though I laughed about it, it really bothered me. I felt like a loser for not being able to understand what the other kids could understand. And I hated people just assuming that I was stupid, even though I was the one saying it the most. After a particularly bad day at school one day, I just had a meltdown and I told my Dad everything about how I felt and how much I hated class and never wanted to go back.

He was great. He listened to me and then suggested that I get some extra help to figure out why exactly I was having such a hard time. And that was amazing. It's not like I became a math genius overnight, but the extra help really showed me that I wasn't stupid, I just learned in a different way. And I didn't feel so powerless anymore.

— C

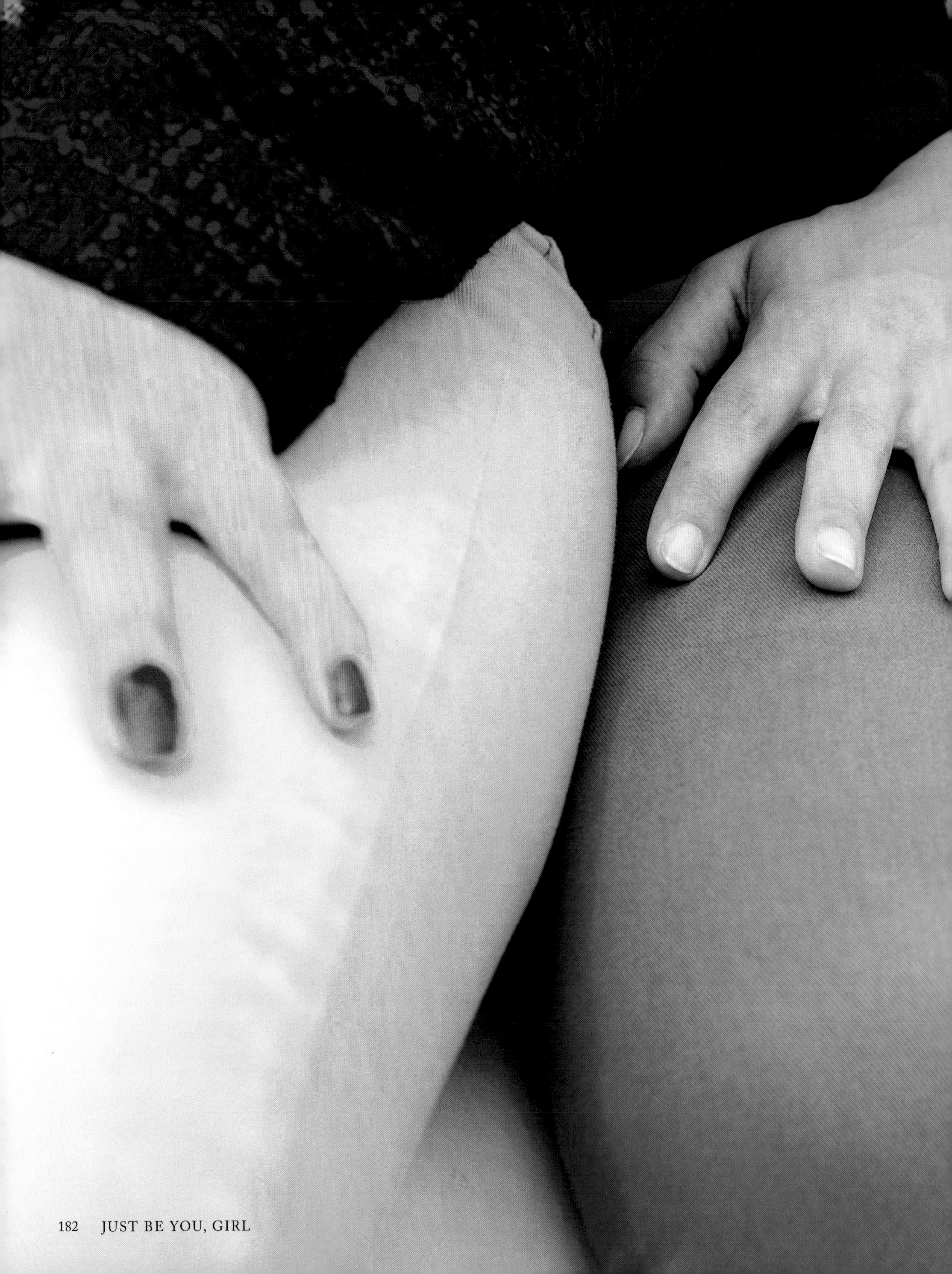

PAY IT FORWARD

It's been mentioned throughout these pages about the benefits of celebrating the beauty in others. And not to repeat what has already been said (that gets boring), I would like to add this.

There are a lot of girls in the world who suffer from low self-esteem. It might not be obvious to you at first because their issues might not be the same as yours, and **let's face it, we all assume that our problems are the worst**. If we think that we have a weight problem, we just automatically assume that thinner girls have nothing to complain about. But that is not how the world works. That beautiful girl in math class might feel ashamed that she can't afford what the other girls in school have, or that popular track star may cry herself to sleep over feelings of worthlessness because someone actually told her she was worthless.

Self-esteem issues can come from anywhere — appearance, abilities, financial, family — anywhere. The point is you can never assume that just because someone has what you value that they are happy.

So what is the point of this discussion? The point is to keep your eyes open, not only to the issues that you are facing, but also to what other girls may be facing. It is not always obvious how other girls are feeling or where their actions are coming from, so you just have to assume that everyone can always use a word of encouragement or a kind gesture. Think of it as a gift that you give to one girl that she can pass on to another girl. Because the sooner we all stop competing with one another and start encouraging each other, the sooner we will all feel a little more comfortable being ourselves.

NOTE: One of the girls I spoke with wanted me to make sure that I included that it is never too late to say you are sorry if you feel that maybe you weren't that fair when judging another.

GIVE YOURSELF TIME

And last, but not least — don't expect to get it right all at once or all the time. You, as I, are amazing — but we are works in progress until the day we die. Sometimes we make bad decisions, sometimes we dump on ourselves or others, sometimes we give up too soon and sometimes we just can't quite find the right path. But that is okay.

It may be hard to be happy with yourself all of the time and that's okay. You just want to keep working towards tipping the balance in your favor.

So forgive yourself any setbacks you may experience and focus on what the future holds.

And remember, sometimes the path you set out on will take some time to yield results, so you have to be patient.

But most of all, always know that you are a truly incredible young woman.

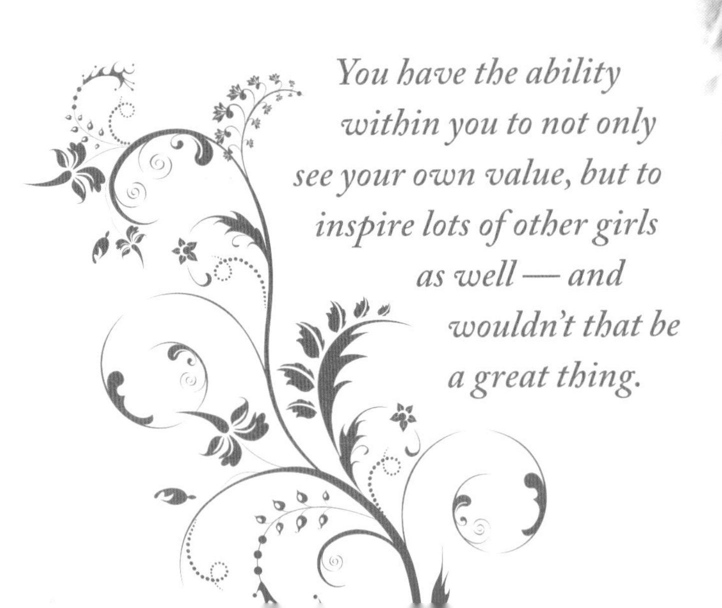

You have the ability within you to not only see your own value, but to inspire lots of other girls as well — and wouldn't that be a great thing.

ENDNOTES

Intro

1. Dove Self-Esteem Fund: "Real Girls, Real Pressure: A National Report on the State of Self-Esteem" (Commissioned: June 2008).

Your Power

1. Dove: *Beyond Stereotypes: Rebuilding the Foundation of Beauty Beliefs.* Findings of the 2005 Dove Global Study (released February 2006).
2. Ibid.
3. Public Health Agency of Canada, *The Health of Canada's Young People: A Mental Health Focus* at *www.phac-aspc.gc.ca.*
4. *The Penguin English Reference Dictionary* (2007).
5. Mayo Clinic at *mayoclinic.org*.
6. Dove Self-Esteem Fund: "Real Girls, Real Pressure: A National Report on the State of Self-Esteem" (Commissioned: June 2008).

Beauty — Through Time and Across Oceans

1. Abigail Howorth, "Forced to Be Fat" in *Marie Claire* magazine, July 2011.
2. "Mauritania: Force-Feeding on Decline but More Dangerous" and "Mauritania: Beauty's Big Problem," Nouakchott, June 26, 2009 (IRIN: Humanitarian news and analysis) at *irinnews.org*.
3. "Karo Tribe" (Omo Valley in Ethiopia) at *Omovalley.com*; and Anouk Zijlma, "Karo Women, Omo River Region, Ethiopia" at *Goafrica.about.com*.
4. "The Origins of Ta Moko," The Museum of New Zealand at *tepapa.govt.nz*; "Maori Culture" at *newzealand.com*; "The Rise of the Maori Tribal Tattoo," BBC News Magazine, September 2011; Steve Theunissen, *The Maori of New Zealand* (Lerner Publishing Group, 2003).
5. Louisa Kim, "Painful Memories for China's Foot-binding Survivors," at *npr.org*, March 2007, and see *www.bbc.co.uk/dna/ptop/alabaster/A1155872.*
6. Penguin English Reference Dictionary.

Marketing Madness

1. *Dictionary.reference.com.*
2. Dove: "Beyond Stereotypes: Rebuilding the Foundation of Beauty Beliefs" findings of the 2005 Dove Global Study (released February 2006).
3. "What's Wrong with Our Bodies Anyway?" *Plus Magazine*, January 2012 at *Plusmodelmag.com.*
4. At *raderprograms.com/causes-statistics/media-eating-disorders.html.*
5. "Diseases and Conditions: Obesity: Symptoms" at *mayoclinic.org*; and "Nutrition Source: Measuring Fat" at *hsph.harvard.edu.*
6. At *jezebel.com/new-york-fashion-week-diversity-talks-but-white-faces-1522416724/1524553069/+dodai.*
7. The Associated Press, "New Israeli Law Bans Underweight Models in Ads," March 20, 2012.

Friends, Frienemies and Foes

1. *Journal of Personality and Social Psychology*, "Self-Esteem Development from Age 14-30 Years: A Longitudinal Study" (2011).
2. Dove Self-Esteem Fund: "Real Girls, Real Pressure: A National Report on the State of Self-Esteem" (Commissioned: June 2008).

Technology, the Media & You

1. Association of Bridal Consultants, "Wedding Cost Statistics," January 1, 2014 at *statisticbrain.com.*

Caution: Danger Ahead

1. At *mayoclinic.org.*
2. *Ibid.*
3. *Ibid.*
4. *Ibid.*

THE THANK YOU PAGE

I hope that you enjoyed *Just Be You, Girl.* I can honestly tell you that I really enjoyed working on it. But like with so many things in life, I could not have done it without a lot of help from a lot of people. And this is where I get to say thank you to all those people.

It would be impossible for me to list in this space every person who has supported this project, whether through a piece of advice, a constructive critique or just a word of encouragement. I am the first to admit to how lucky I am to have such great people in my life, people who were willing to sit down for a coffee and discuss ideas, or review manuscripts or answer questions. The more so as many of these people were not known to me previously, but were still willing to take the time when I asked for help. It's amazing the generosity people will show when asked and, for this, I am so grateful.

I am also grateful to all the young women who so graciously shared their stories with me so that I could share them with you. The struggles surrounding these issues can be overwhelming, especially when we feel that we are alone in our thoughts. So sharing our stories, our insecurities as well as our triumphs is such an amazing way to offer support to someone in need. So thank you to everyone who shared your stories with me, and I encourage every girl to use her voice to help another.

I would also like to thank my wonderful editor Catherine Leek. Now, I am completely new to publishing, so I am not exactly sure of everything that editors are supposed to do, but I am pretty sure that Catherine went above and beyond. Thank you Catherine, not only for your amazing editing skills but also for guiding me through each step of this process. You not only kept the work on track, but offered me unyielding encouragement when the project seemed to get a little too daunting. And you did it all with such kindness and patience. Thank you so much.

And thank you to Kim Monteforte. Kim is the woman responsible for making this book look so beautiful. I said, "Kim, it can't look like a textbook" and voilà. Kim worked her considerable talent and I think made the book look amazing (if I do say so myself). Kim, thank you for creating something even more beautiful than I could have imagined.

On a more personal note, I would like to thank the two people in my life who have inspired me the most.

To my Mom and Dad, who always taught my siblings and me, both through words and example, that women and men are equal in all ways. We learnt early that our voices should be heard and that our value as a person is determined by the type of person we are and not by anything superficial. We were always taught that we had the choice to live our lives as we wanted as long as we respected others and ourselves. Thank you so much Mom and Dad. I love you Mom. I miss you Dad.

My parents forged a strong family bond between me and my siblings. I probably didn't really appreciate this until I was older and realized how much easier it is to find your own strength when you are surrounded by such a loving support system. So I would like to acknowledge how much this has meant to me and how important my sister and brothers are to giving me the confidence to share my voice. Thank you Kevin, Rita and Michael — I couldn't have asked for better siblings if I got to pick you myself.

And to my husband Mike, what can I possibly say that would convey my feelings? I can't think of a thing I have done in the past half of my life without you by my side offering help and encouragement. Without you there would definitely be no book. When I told you that I wanted to do this, even though I had never done anything of the kind before, you didn't even bat an eye. Your unwavering support is amazing. Your practical help is indispensable. And your humor just makes the whole thing fun. You really are my best friend. Thank you so much for everything.

And of course, to the two people who have added more to my life than I could have ever dreamed and who, through their intelligence and insight, continue to expand my world. To my beautiful boy Sam, thank you for patiently listening to more discussions on female issues than anyone has a right to expect from an adolescent boy. You make me laugh and you make me proud! And to my daughter Keeley — you are such an incredible young woman. Your intelligence challenges me (in a good way) and your spirit lifts me. I love you both so much.

And lastly, I would like to acknowledge that I know that much of what is contained within these pages is not new. I have not "discovered" or "revolutionized" ideas in this area. This book highlights the knowledge and experience of many, brought together in the hopes of offering one more avenue of support to young girls who face these issues. If we continue to share these ideas through books, movies, song, art or just discussion, then the conversation can only get stronger. And that can only be a good thing.

If you would like to continue talking or share your thoughts or stories, please visit *Justbeyougirl.com*.

Me and my daughter, Keeley.

Carolyn McMahon, herself a former young girl, now has a beautiful young daughter of her own. New to writing, *Just Be You, Girl* was born from the endless discussions Carolyn has had with her daughter surrounding the issues of self-esteem and the need for a strong self-image.

Written specifically to speak directly to young girls, Carolyn's aim is to address the everyday issues and influences that can affect how a young girl sees herself.

Conversational in style, *Just Be You, Girl* strives not only to educate, but also to provide some comfort and guidance to young girls struggling with issues of self-esteem and poor body image.

In addition to utilizing the knowledge gained from her own background in marketing and advertising, Carolyn draws on available research as well as the common-sense guidance of many of the women in her own life and beyond.

For more information, discussion or feedback, please visit *justbeyougirl.com.*